TRIFFIC
CHOCOLATE

The Knowledge

TRIFFIC CHOCOLATE

by Alan MacDonald

Illustrated by
Clive Goddard

This edition produced for the Book People Ltd,
Hall Wood Avenue, Haydock, St Helens WA11 9UL

First published in the UK by Scholastic Ltd, 2000
Text copyright © Alan MacDonald, 2000
Illustrations copyright © Clive Goddard, 2000
Extract from ETIQUETTE FOR CHOCOLATE LOVERS by Beryl Peters.
Copyright Beryl Peters, Copper Beech Publishing Ltd, reproduced by permission.

ISBN 0 439 95406 1

All rights reserved
Typeset by TW Typesetting, Midsomer Norton, Somerset
Printed and bound by Nørhaven Paperback A/S, Denmark

The right of Alan MacDonald and Clive Goddard to be identified as the
author and illustrator of this work respectively has been asserted by them
in accordance with the Copyright, Designs and Patents Act, 1988.

CONTENTS

INTRODUCTION

Chocolate. Is there any other word in the English language that commands such attention? Produce a packet of Rolos and you'll instantly have lots of new friends. Rustle a box of chocolates and adults will miraculously wake from their slumber in front of the TV. Ask for a bite of someone's Mars bar and watch the look of horror on their face. Nothing else has the same effect as chocolate.

Think about it, would you...

Of course not. Chocolate is unique and people have known that from the start. From the first discovery of chocolate people went nuts over the sweet stuff. It wasn't just that they liked it. They loved it, had to have more. And so the sweet that started from a bean in Central America, gradually conquered the whole world. Today the chances are you're never more than a short stroll away from a bar of chocolate. (Unless you happen to be in the Sahara Desert, of course.)

This book is for any dedicated chocophile who'd like to know more about their favourite food. In it you can follow the nutty history of chocolate from Aztecs to Aero. You can meet famous chocolate lovers like Samuel Pepys, Queen Victoria and Roald Dahl and learn why chocolate was also a favourite with poisoners. And while you're about it, you can impress your family and friends with hundreds of choctastic facts from our Triffic trivia files.

It's all true and it's all in this book. So give yourself a treat and dip into the strange, surprising and sumptuously sticky world of chocolate.

IT STARTED WITH A BEAN

First things first. What is chocolate?

Stupid question. We all know what chocolate is. It's that sticky stuff you find on your jeans when you're leaving the cinema.

Actually it's not such a daft question as it sounds. Experts have been arguing for years over what can be correctly called chocolate and what can't. In fact, some European countries think that the sweet stuff we eat in Britain shouldn't be called chocolate at all (but more of that later).

To put it simply, chocolate is a food that comes from the seeds of the tropical cacao tree.

BEANS MEANS CHOCOLATE!

Did you spot that the word "cacao" is cocoa with a spelling mistake? In fact, it's the other way round – cocoa is the spelling mistake.

Cacao is a Spanish word which comes from the Aztec *cacahuatl*. The error of calling it cocoa was probably made by English traders centuries ago who would have got 0 out of 10 in any spelling test. They brought cacao beans back to England and introduced them as cocoa beans.

If you want to be a clever dick you can try this fascinating fact on your family.

The chocolate you get from the shop is nearly always milk chocolate. But actually there are lots of different types of chocolate. Beware though, some of it isn't proper choccie at all. See if you can spot which of the ones below *cannot* be counted as chocolate.

Spot the fake

1. Dark or plain chocolate
Dark chocolate is bitter-tasting, strong chocolate containing around 50% chocolate liquor. It's serious chocolate for serious chocophiles who hate caramel, wafer or anything else messing up the purity of their beloved chocolate.

2. Unsweetened chocolate
Cooled down pure chocolate liquor which is a favourite with chefs who make yummy choccie puds. It's also the stuff that you see on top of cakes in curly shavings.

10

3. Semi-sweet chocolate
Again, mainly used for cooking. It has extra cocoa butter and sugar added to the chocolate liquor.

4. Milk chocolate
This is the stuff that most of us desire on a daily basis. It doesn't take an Einstein to know that milk chocolate has got milk added to it. But it also has extra cocoa butter, sugar and vanilla. It's mainly useful for wolfing down in large quantities.

5. White chocolate
Contains cocoa butter, sugar, milk and vanilla but no cocoa solids. This gives it a white or beige colour.

6. Confectioner's chocolate
Sometimes used for covering cakes or strawberries. A chocolate-flavoured candy that melts easily and hardens quickly.

Answers: 5. and **6.** are *not* counted as chocolate. Although white chocolate is called chocolate it doesn't have any cocoa solids in it. It may look nice, and taste creamy but, sorry, it isn't real chocolate. (Maybe it should be called creamolate?) The same goes for confectioner's chocolate, which is just a sort of chocolate-coloured candy. It may look a bit like chocolate but then, let's face it, so does a muddy puddle.

From bean to bar

So now we know what chocolate is and what it isn't, how is chocolate actually made? Can you just get hold of a few cocoa beans, plant them in your garden and harvest a crop of Kit Kats from a tree in a few years' time? Sadly, it isn't that simple (or else Nestlé would be out of business).

From bean to bar, chocolate has to go through a great many stages. If you're eager to start up your own home-made chocolate business, here's what you'll have to do.

Making chocolate

Stage 1: Grow your own cocoa
You will need:
room for a small plantation
a few thousand cacao seedlings
plenty of comics to read
a long-handled pod-chopper
banana leaves

1. Move to a hot tropical country near the equator (Brazil or West Africa, probably not Wales).

2. Plant your cacao seedlings in the shade of a larger tree, e.g. banana or mango trees (always hard to find in Wales).

3. Wait 12–15 years for the trees to grow and bear their full crop. (Here's where the comics come in handy.)

4. Cut the ripe pods off with your long-handled pod-chopper (basically a knife tied to a pole). Split open the pods and grab the beans.

5. Cover the beans with banana leaves and allow to "ferment" for about a week. They should turn brown and develop their flavour.

6. Leave to dry in the sun for another three days.

Stage 2: Making cocoa mass
You will need:
a cleaning machine
a big oven (not your mum's)
a cracker and fanner
a grinding mill

1. Clean the beans to remove the pulp and other yukky stuff.
2. Roast them at 250°F in a big revolving oven.
3. Crack open the shells and fan them in a current of air to leave the edible cocoa called "nibs".
4. Grind the nibs between rollers to make brown chocolate liquor – cocoa mass – the basis of all chocolate. But it's still gritty and grainy, rather like sand. Which is probably not stuff you'd want to eat.
5. Extract about half the fat (cocoa butter) in a heavy press. Don't throw it away, you'll need it later.

Stage 3: Making milk chocolate
You will need:
sugar
vanilla
milk
a chocolate factory

1. The cocoa mass is mixed with sugar and condensed milk to make a kind of paste.
2. The paste passes through a series of rotating rollers. It comes out the other side as a fine, flaky powder called chocolate crumb. The cocoa butter you saved earlier is added back in to make a paste.
3. Now the "conching" that gives chocolate that melt-in-the-mouth smoothness. The chocolate is heated in huge vats. Giant rollers move slowly over it. This'll take several days, so back to reading your comics.

4. The temperature is slowly reduced so that the chocolate is "tempered". Now for the dreamy part. Watch that liquid chocolate swirling down into metal moulds.
5. The chocolate sets in the mould. At last you can bite into your bar of milk chocolate!
    (Alternatively you may just want to nip down to your local sweetshop and forget the whole thing.)

Chocolate mountain

As we've seen, chocolate takes a whole lot of time and trouble to make. If the silky brown stuff wasn't so scrumptious manufacturers probably wouldn't bother. Except, of course, that chocolate has made companies like Mars, Rowntree-Nestlé and Cadbury very rich.

Huge amounts of chocolate are sold and gobbled up every year. For instance, in the UK we eat over half a million tonnes of chocolate every year. Sales in the 1990s showed that on average in one year each of us was chomping through...

120 chocolate bars
10 bags of chocolates
3·5 lb boxes of chocolates
1·5 Easter eggs
3·5 creme eggs
15·5 mini-creme eggs

That's a mountain of chocolate by any standards. The question is, why do we find chocolate so utterly irresistible? Take an example. It's Christmas Day in your house and everybody's stuffed with too much turkey. Pass round the fruit bowl and no one wants an apple or a banana. But produce a box of chocolates and suddenly your overstuffed relatives are hungry! They're licking their lips and secretly hoping you won't take the caramel one which is their favourite.

Why does chocolate have this effect? Scientists have come up with lots of theories. We asked one of them to explain.

Perhaps all of these theories have a smackerel of truth.

It's true that the *taste* and *smell* of chocolate is unique. A chocolate expert (or choco-buff) savours high-quality chocolate like a vintage wine. She will tell you that a piece of quality chocolate has a perfect balance between sweetness and bitterness. It contains subtle hints of all sorts of things, like new-mown hay, sherry and cheese, that you didn't even realize were in chocolate.

Then again, the *texture* is just as important. Chocolate is unlike any other food. The cocoa butter gives chocolate its smoothness and a slight change in temperature does the rest. A slab of chocolate stays hard in the packet, but pop it in your mouth and the heat is enough to melt the choccie and release its sweet gooey flavours.

Finally there is the claim that chocolate is *addictive*. When people say that Maltesers or M&Ms are moreish, they mean exactly that – they want more!

There are over 300 chemicals in chocolate which could explain this. One is a small amount of caffeine, which is a pick-me-up found in coffee. Other chemicals have names that are a mouthful like phenylethylamine (fenny-lethy-la-meen).

Phenylethylamine has been proven to raise blood pressure and heart rate. It's possible it gives us the "high" that some people claim they get from eating chocolate.

However, some scientists argue that these chemical theories are a load of old hogswoggle. They say we eat chocolate just because it's a nice treat and we like it. Personally, I think they may have a point – and pass the Cadbury's Dairy Milk.

Killjoy critics

If you find something that millions of people enjoy, you can bet that sooner or later someone will start to say it's "a bad thing". In fact, people have been calling chocolate "bad" for hundreds of years. In the seventeenth century clergy went as far as condemning drinking chocolate as "the beverage of Satan". As late as 1712, the English magazine, *The Spectator*, warned:

BE CAREFUL HOW YOU MEDDLE WITH ROMANCE, CHOCOLATE AND THE LIKE INFLAMERS

The sour critics are still around today. Chocolate gets blamed for all sorts of things from giving you spots to making your teeth rot. But are these claims true or are they just a myth invented by the spoilsports?

Now at last you can find out. Try our quiz and sort out the hits from the myths.

Triffic trivia quiz – hit or a myth?

True or False?

① CHOCOLATE IS BAD FOR YOUR TEETH

② CHOCOLATE IS GOOD FOR YOUR TEETH

Answers:

1. True. Choccie bars are bad for your teeth because they contain lots of sugar.

But don't despair because…

2. True. Chocolate is also good for your teeth! French doctor, Hervé Robert claims: "Cocoa contains at least three substances which kill the bacteria which lead to the formation of dental plaque." He points out that dentists say that eating grapes, bananas or bread are all more likely to cause tooth decay than scoffing chocolate!

I SHOULD CUT DOWN ON THE FRUIT A BIT…

3. False. Surveys carried out in America have found no connection between eating chocs and getting spots.

4. False. There's no proof that eating chocolate by itself causes headaches or migraine. If you were silly enough to scoff chocolate after bingeing on soft cheese and red wine, *then* you might get a thumping headache.

5. True. OK, chocolate is high in calories which make you fat. But don't despair, there may be a way round this one. High-quality chocolate (with 50% cocoa solids) contains less fat than the ordinary choc bars on sale at your local sweet shop. And since you'd have to walk a long way to find a shop that sells high-quality chocolate you'd also be burning off lots of calories on the journey. So in the end you see, chocolate should be part of any sensible diet!

6. True. Chocolate is high in healthy stuff like nutrients and vitamins. Ask the space scientists at NASA in America. They invested a lot of money in chocolate research and came to the conclusion that chocolate is the perfect high-energy, nutritious food.

7. True! Now you have the perfect answer to any teacher who wants to confiscate your Mars bar. British scientists in 1997 discovered that a quarter of girls at secondary school were not taking enough iron in their diet which led to a slump in their brain-power. The solution? Eat chocolate! (OK, they did also mention things like lamb's liver, wholemeal bread and green vegetables.)

Blowing hot or cold

Assuming you like chocolate (after all, you *are* reading this book), what's the best way to keep it? There are a number of possible solutions:

Remember, the key factor in choosing a safe place for your chocolate stash is temperature. Chocolate is very fussy about temperature. It doesn't like to be too hot or too cold – like Goldilocks in the fairytale it prefers to be "just right". Here's how you can expect chocolate to behave as its temperature changes.

To nibble or to gobble?

In this chapter we've just unwrapped chocolate and got to know it a little better. What it is, where it comes from, how it's made, why it's good for us and how to store it. There is of course one thing missing. Surely you're thinking, the whole point of chocolate is to *eat it*.

There are lots of ways to eat chocolate. You can nibble it politely, slobber over it rudely or just wolf it down in seconds. On the other hand you could find new recipes for cooking and eating chocolate. Of course recipes for chocolate cake or chocolate puddings are ten a penny. In this book we've searched the world to offer you something different, you might even say downright weird.

Weird recipes: chocolate spaghetti

The original recipe for this dish is a carefully kept secret. But this is one chef's suggestion.

Ingredients:
12 g of margarine
2 tablespoons of castor sugar
2 tablespoons of cocoa
vanilla essence
100 g of spaghetti in 5 cm pieces

Method:
1. Boil a litre of water in a large saucepan with 1 level teaspoon of salt.
2. Cook the spaghetti until it's tender. If it's overcooked it'll glue together in a mass.
3. Drain in a colander and pour boiling water over to separate the pieces.
4. Warm the rest of the ingredients in a pan and mix well.
5. Put in the spaghetti and stir until it's coated in sticky chocolate spread.
6. Allow to cool and load into your mouth with a fork.

600–1600 The age of froth

AD 600 The Mayan Indians establish the first known cocoa plantations in Central America. The secret of cocoa has already been around for hundreds of years.

1000 The Maya use cocoa beans as money and as a way of counting.

1200 Chocolate wars. The Aztecs conquer the Mayas, who are forced to pay their taxes in cocoa beans.

1502 Columbus brings cocoa beans back to Europe. Ferdinand, King of Spain, turns his nose up at them.

1513 A Spaniard reports he bought a slave in Mexico for 100 cocoa beans.

1519 Spanish adventurer, Hernan Cortés lands in Mexico and slurps his first cup of Aztec frothy chocolate.

1528 Conquering Cortés brings the bean back to Europe with the recipe for making drinking chocolate.
1528–1650s The sneaky Spaniards keep chocolate a secret for over a century.

The drink of the gods

"Chocolate is an invention so noble that it should be the invention of the gods." Paris, 1684

Did you know there was once a chocolate bar named Aztec? It was made by Cadbury but sadly was taken off the market in 1978 because of poor sales. (In 1999 Cadbury brought out a special limited edition Aztec 2000 bar as a tribute to the gone but not forgotten Aztec.) Probably few people who ever chewed an Aztec bar knew it was a tribute to the civilization who gave chocolate to the world.

The Aztecs were great chocoholics but they weren't actually the first to go nuts for chocolate. In fact they cadged their cocoa beans from a tribe called the Maya. For hundreds of years the Maya had been growing their own cocoa beans in Central America. They used them not only to make chocolate but also to count. In primitive Mexican pictures a basket of 8,000 cocoa beans represents the figure 8,000. So early Mayan maths lessons may have looked a bit like this.

Chocolate coins

If the Maya were pretty keen on cocoa, the Aztecs were crazy about it. When the Aztecs conquered the Maya they forced them to pay taxes (or tributes) in cocoa beans. Maybe this is where we get the saying "I haven't got a bean." The Maya probably tried that one on their Aztec rulers many a time.

In fact, cocoa beans were so valuable the Aztecs treated them just like hard cash. If you had a pocketful of beans you could buy a lot. For instance:

If you ask your mum or dad for a new bike/CD/ computer game they'll often come out with the same old tired excuse. But now, thanks to the Aztecs, you've got the perfect answer.

Hearts and chocolates

The Aztecs treated cocoa almost like gold itself. Dogs that had a cocoa-coloured spot on them were highly honoured as it was thought they would ensure a good harvest.

COCOA SPOT DOG –
GOOD LUCK OMEN

DALMATION DOG –
NO USE AT ALL

Cocoa beans were used in all kinds of ways. Not only as money, but also as gifts at a child's birth or as an offering to the gods. The Aztecs had dozens of gods and they were a pretty bloodthirsty bunch. One of the things the gods were keen on (besides chocolate) was human sacrifice.

(*NB You may like to skip this next part if you're a bit squeamish.*)

The Aztecs believed that if they didn't sacrifice some poor soul to the gods every day then some pretty major disasters would befall them...

1. The sun wouldn't rise the next morning.

2. The maize which was their staple diet would stop growing.

3. The world itself would come to an end.

Faced with wipe-out, what would you have done? You can bet the Aztecs kept their gods happy with daily sacrifices. Often they used captives from other tribes. Feast days were a particularly jolly occasion when thousands would be slaughtered and their still-beating hearts removed and offered to the sun god, Huitzilopochtli.

Scum of the earth

Turning to a more tasteful subject, what about the chocolate? You may imagine hordes of happy Aztecs went around munching chocolate bars like we do today – at least until it was their turn to keep the gods happy. In fact, the kind of chocolate the Aztecs enjoyed was liquid chocolate. It would be another 700 years before solid chocolate was invented.

The Aztec drink wasn't a bit like the hot chocolate we drink today. The Aztecs called it *xocoatl*, which means bitter water. One legend says that when the cocoa beans were stirred with water in huge vats over a fire, the mixture made a "choco-choco" sound as it bubbled, which gave us the word chocolate. This story is about as reliable as a smiling Aztec who invites you to dinner. It's much more likely that the word chocolate comes from the Aztec word *choqui* meaning warmth.

Xocoatl was actually served cold but it had a spicy bitter taste due to some of the weird ingredients – such as hot chilli peppers!

It was a reddish colour with a frothy scum floating on top. No doubt you're dying to taste it already, so here's the recipe – as passed on in the words of an unknown Spanish soldier.

Weird recipe: Aztec frothy chocolate – the drink with a kick

Ingredients:
cacao seeds - chilli peppers - cinnamon
cloves - cornmeal - water

Method:

1. These seeds which are called cacao are ground and made into powder and other small seeds are ground, and this powder is put into certain basins.

2. Then they [the Aztecs] put water on it and mix it with a spoon. And after having mixed it very well they change it from one basin to another, so that a foam is raised which they put in a bowl made for the purpose.

3. And when they wish to drink it, they mix it with certain small spoons of gold or silver or wood, and drink it, and drinking it one must open one's mouth, because being foam one must give it room to subside, and go down bit by bit.

This drink is the healthiest thing and the greatest sustenance of anything you could drink in the world. He who drinks a cup of this liquid can go a whole day without eating anything else.

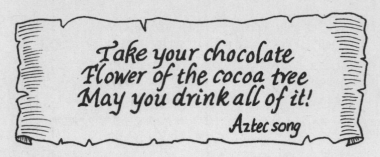

Chocolate conquerors – the Spanish invasion

You probably know it was Christopher Columbus who discovered the New World of America. But did you know that Columbus was also the first European to discover chocolate? Unfortunately, the great discoverer didn't know a good thing when he saw one. Instead of rushing home to open his own chocolate factory, he presented the precious cocoa seeds to the King of Spain, who didn't care a bean for them.

It happened on Columbus's fourth voyage in 1502. Landing on an island called Guanaja, Columbus sent a search party ashore on 16 August. They immediately captured a Maya trading canoe, rowed by slaves with ropes round their necks. The canoes' cargo contained not only cotton, clothes and war clubs but something much more precious. Columbus's second son, Ferdinand, described it as:

...THOSE ALMONDS WHICH IN NEW SPAIN (MEXICO) ARE USED FOR MONEY. THEY SEEMED TO HOLD THESE ALMONDS AT GREAT PRICE, FOR WHEN THEY WERE BROUGHT ON BOARD SHIP TOGETHER WITH THEIR GOODS, I OBSERVED THAT WHEN ANY OF THESE ALMONDS FELL, THEY ALL STOOPED TO PICK IT UP, AS IF AN EYE HAD FALLEN

Ferdinand had no idea that these "almonds" were actually the cacao fruit which, you remember, is the source of chocolate. No wonder the Maya stooped to pick them up: no one in their right mind drops their chocolate and leaves it on the ground!

Poor Columbus died four years later without ever knowing the pleasure of tasting chocolate. It was left to another adventurer to make the discovery.

Cunning Cortés

The credit for introducing chocolate to Europe goes to another Spaniard, some twenty years later. Hernan Cortés was a fortune-seeking soldier attracted to Mexico by stories of gold and jewels. He had no idea when he set sail from Cuba that the greatest treasure he'd bring back was chocolate.

Cortés landed in 1519 with a tiny force of 550 men, 16 horses and a few cannons. How could he possibly hope to conquer the mighty Aztec empire with such an army? It's one of the most amazing stories in history. Luck, superstition and dirty dealing all played a part. But perhaps if we could take a peek at his secret diary, Cortés would have told his own version of the tale.

Diary of a chocolate soldier

1519 21 April   Landed on the coast of this land they call Mexico. The natives we've met so far are scared to death of us. They've never seen white men before and gaze at our horses as if they are giant, four-legged monsters. Of course, they've never seen a cannon breathing fire either. I soon gave them a demonstration which sent them running for their lives! Conquering this country will be a pushover!

BOOM!

22 April   Messengers arrive from Montezuma, the king of the Aztecs, bringing gold and silver. If he thinks he can buy us off and send us home, he's a fool. The sight of all that gleaming gold only makes me more determined to plunder the fabulous wealth of this land.

Rumours say Montezuma is a god who eats the hearts of his own people. Ordered our boats to be burnt to make sure none of my cowardly crew has the chance to run. (Naturally I buried the metal frames so we can dig them up and rebuild the boats later. You don't think I'm stupid, do you?)

'7 November   Finally arrived at Tenochtitlan, the Aztecs' capital city. We can see the mighty walls and temples of the royal city on an isle in the middle of a mighty lake. Our cannons are loaded, our muskets primed. I expect a great battle tomorrow.

8 November   Caramba! Instead of fighting us, Montezuma has welcomed us like gods! A great banquet was spread in our honour with dishes of wild duck, turkey and rabbit. The king is served goblets of pure gold with a bitter drink made from the cocoa plant. (They say he takes it before visiting his wives.) I saw a good fifty large jugs of this frothy xocoatl. The Aztecs prize it highly and only offer it to warriors and honoured guests (women aren't allowed a sniff of it).

Montezuma appears to fear and honour me above all men. This could work in our favour!

The god of chocolate

Maybe Cortés guessed at the reason for his big welcome. On his travels through Mexico he'd gained the help of a woman called Donna Marina who'd explained to him the ancient Aztec legend of one of the gods. Quetzalcoatl was the feathered serpent god who could do smart things like breathe life into stones. In human form he was also an Aztec king. It was Quetzalcoatl who brought the seeds of the cacao tree to earth. As far as the Aztecs were concerned he was the god of chocolate.

Long ago Quetzalcoatl had left his people, promising he'd come back one day. The year predicted for his return was 1519, which just happened to be the year Cortés appeared with his horses and fire-breathing cannons. Poor Montezuma mistook the greedy Spanish soldier for an Aztec god. (After all, anyone can make a mistake.)

By the time the mistake dawned on Montezuma it was too late. Cortés repaid the king's hospitality by taking him hostage. For months cunning Cortés and his small army ruled the Aztec city – helping themselves to the king's personal storehouse of 960 million cocoa beans. (The king's guard alone drank 2,000 jugs of foamy chocolate a day.)

At last, in May 1520, there was an uprising against the Spanish invaders. Cortés and his army were thrown out of the city, but Montezuma was mysteriously killed in the fighting. A year later

Cortés returned with a stronger army and the city fell after a 75-day siege. It was the end of the line for the great empire of the Aztecs and the beginning of chocolate's journey across the world.

Cortés – who was made governor of Mexico – knew a good thing when he saw one. He didn't forget the bitter drink he'd tasted at Montezuma's table, and made great claims for the powers of chocolate.

Cortés is known as the man who brought chocolate to Spain and therefore introduced it to the rest of the world. There is no proof of this, but certainly chocolate arrived in Spain in the 1530s along with other wonders from the New World such as avocado pears, tomatoes, vanilla and turkeys.

Charles V, King of Spain, didn't take long to go nuts over triffic chocolate.

Yummy or scummy?

Yet not all Europeans in the sixteenth century were queuing up to sing the praises of chocolate. Some who encountered it in the New World held their noses and stuck out their tongues.

IT SEEMED MORE A DRINK FOR PIGS THAN A DRINK FOR HUMANITY

Girolomo Benzoni, Italian historian and adventurer, 1575

IT DISGUSTS THOSE WHO ARE NOT USED TO IT FOR IT HAS A FOAM ON TOP OR A SCUM LIKE BUBBLING

Jose de Acosta, Jesuit, 1590

A scummy pig-swill doesn't sound like a promising start for a delicacy that would one day take the world by storm. Yet experiments with the dark beans had already started. Once chocolate reached the Spanish court it started to take on a new taste. Instead of cold frothy chocolate, the Spanish preferred their chocolate hot. And instead of adding chilli pepper to burn the mouth, they added sugar to sweeten it. Many other ingredients would be ground, added and mixed before chocolate would become the mouth-watering, melting stuff we eat today.

Triffic trivia

Did you know?

1. The cacao tree is "cauliflorous" (nothing to do with cauliflower!). This means that its small white flowers and seed pods grow straight out from the trunk rather than from young leafy stems as is usual in European trees.

2. Chocolate really is divine. The botanical name for the cacao tree – Theobroma Cacao – means "the food of the gods".

3. Plain chocolate contains more sugar than milk chocolate.

4. Nine out of ten Brits eat chocolate on a regular basis.

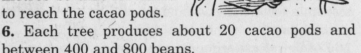

5. A cacao tree can grow 10–13 metres high but most are pruned to 7 metres so that it's easier to reach the cacao pods.

6. Each tree produces about 20 cacao pods and between 400 and 800 beans.

7. Monkeys, squirrels and woodpeckers are all enemies of chocolate. They eat cacao pods or damage the young plants.

8. Midges, on the other hand, are chocolate's best friends. They help to pollinate the cacao plants.

9. Chocolate by-products are used to make all kinds of things such as lipstick, cooking fat, soap and fertilizer.

10. The Maya were so fond of chocolate that they used it to baptize their children.

CHOCOLATE CONQUERS EUROPE

1560–1800
Healthy chocolate

1569 The great chocolate debate – is it a food or a drink? Pope Pius V declares chocolate doesn't break the Lenten fast.

1655 Britain captures Jamaica and joins the scramble for colonies – and cocoa beans.

1657 The first chocolate house opens in London (run by a Frenchman), but only the rich can afford to drink chocolate in it.

1660 Louis XIV of France marries Spanish Princess Maria Theresa who brings her own cocoa beans. Drinking chocolate is soon all the rage at the French court.

1674 The first eating chocolate is served in a London coffee house – chocolate cakes and rolls "in the Spanish style".

41

1685 English gentlemen take hot chocolate for breakfast and it's recommended as part of a healthy diet.

1697 The mayor of Zurich drinks chocolate in Brussels and hotfoots back to Switzerland with the news.

1700s The slave trade flourishes. But cocoa workers' lives aren't worth a bean.

1720 Italian chocolateers are famed all over Europe and visit France, Germany and Switzerland.

1765 America gets the chocolate bug late. The first chocolate factory in the USA opens in Massachusetts.

1791 Napoleon takes a regular cup of chocolate while staying in London.

1810 Venezuela in South America produces half the world's cocoa. One third is still swallowed up by the sweet-toothed Spanish.

In the Aztec empire chocolate was a drink for kings and warriors with their feathered headdresses. When chocolate reached Europe nothing much changed.

It was still only the bigwigs in society who got the chance to taste the magical brew. Poor people didn't get their hands on chocolate until the revolution of the nineteenth century when people like the Cadbury brothers started mass-producing it.

During the seventeenth and eighteenth centuries chocolate conquered Europe. It started in Spain where it got stuck for a century, but once the word was out chocolate's fame spread quickly through France, Italy, England and – eventually – back to America.

The secretive Spaniards

Spain kept the secret of chocolate to itself for almost a hundred years. English pirates did capture a haul of cocoa beans when they plundered a Spanish ship in 1579. But they burned the whole cargo thinking it was nothing but sheep's droppings.

THEY DON'T SMELL LIKE SHEEP'S DROPPINGS

The Spanish meanwhile went about perfecting their own recipe for drinking chocolate. They were soon adding all kinds of ingredients – sugar, vanilla, cinnamon, almonds and hazelnuts – to make the bitter water more drinkable. The Spanish expected their servants to spend up to half an hour preparing their hot chocolate to perfection. Maybe that was half the appeal. What chocolate doesn't taste better when you have to wait for it?

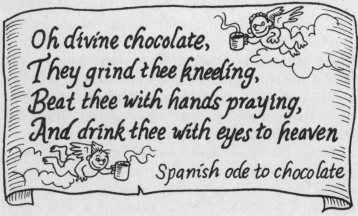

Oh divine chocolate,
They grind thee kneeling,
Beat thee with hands praying,
And drink thee with eyes to heaven

Spanish ode to chocolate

It's all a long way from today where we simply open a tin of hot chocolate and sprinkle a couple of spoonfuls into some hot milk.

It's odd that the Spaniards needed an excuse to drink chocolate. It wasn't enough that it tasted good, they had to convince themselves that chocolate was *healthy*. Chocolate was promoted as a medicine which had marvellous benefits. Many doctors said it was healthy, sustaining and aided the digestion. None of this could be proved or disproved, but it gave people a welcome excuse to drink the stuff.

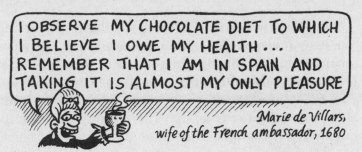

I OBSERVE MY CHOCOLATE DIET TO WHICH I BELIEVE I OWE MY HEALTH... REMEMBER THAT I AM IN SPAIN AND TAKING IT IS ALMOST MY ONLY PLEASURE

Marie de Villars, wife of the French ambassador, 1680

Flying cups and stable saucers

Drinking your chocolate at court was another matter. Remember this was the age of potty wigs, powdered faces and courtly manners. To sip your chocolate while making witty conversation and bowing or curtsying at the right moment was no easy thing. At first aristocrats drank their chocolate from a small bowl called a *jicara*. This occasionally led to accidents.

The Viceroy of Peru, the Marques de Mancera, was horrified one day to see a lady actually *spill* a bowl of chocolate down her dress. To avoid the repeat of such a disaster he invented a new way of drinking chocolate. Mancera dreamed up the cup and saucer! His idea was a saucer with a ring in the middle to hold the cup steady. He modestly named his new invention a *mancerina* after himself. It was soon a smash hit all over Europe.

Say goodbye to the misery of chocolate stains with new Mancerina

The great chocolate debate

Yet even armed with a *mancerina* there was still one obstacle to enjoying your chocolate. As chocolate grew in popularity it attracted the attention of the church. This raised a ticklish problem – was chocolate a food or a drink? This may seem a nutty question since solid eating chocolate hadn't yet been invented. But critics pointed out that all sorts of stuff, such as eggs or breadcrumbs, was added to drinking chocolate. Since chocolate also provided enough nourishment to keep hunger away, didn't that make it a food?

Who cared anyway? Well, Catholics did because if chocolate was a food then it should be banned during the 40 days of Lent when Christians were meant to fast (go without food). Since nearly every Spaniard was a Catholic it was a hot issue. In 1569 Pope Pius V was served a cup of chocolate and chocoholics everywhere held their breath to see what he would say.

Luckily the Pope thought it was disgusting. He was certain that no one would want to drink such a foul brew anyway. This, however, didn't satisfy many church scholars. For over two hundred years the arguments raged back and forth without the question being settled.

Death by chocolate

Whether chocolate was a food or a drink it soon became popular for a nastier reason. Murderers discovered that it was the perfect drink in which to slip their victims a dose of poison. The chocolate's strong taste meant the victim couldn't taste the bitter poison – or if they did it was too late. Since its invention chocolate has claimed a number of famous victims.

1. The nobbled noble

A noble at the French court of Louis XIII was said to be devoted to chocolate and improving its quality. So when he jilted a lady of noble birth she planned a fitting revenge. Inviting him to her house, she offered him a cup of chocolate into which she slipped a deadly poison. The noble drained the chocolate to the last drop and the poison began to do its work. Before he died, the noble drew his killer to him and breathed his last words:

THE CHOCOLATE WOULD HAVE BEEN BETTER IF YOU'D ADDED A LITTLE MORE SUGAR; THE POISON GIVES IT A BITTER FLAVOUR...UUH!

2. A chocolate Charlie

According to rumours, King Charles II of England (1660–1689) was another victim of death by chocolate. People claimed his mistress, the scheming Duchess of Portsmouth, poisoned him with a cup of spiked choccie.

This was a good story but it's probably absolute twaddle. It's more likely the king died of a kidney disease – though he probably didn't do himself much good rubbing the dust of Egyptian mummies into his body. The right royal Charlie believed their greatness would rub off on him.

SERVES HIM RIGHT!

3. The poisoned Pope

When Pope Clement XIV died in 1774 foul play was suspected. Sir Horace Mann wrote in a letter that "the murder of the Pope has been proved by the clearest evidence." Apparently the Pope's fingernails had dropped off: a sure sign that poison was mixed up in the case. According to Mann, the Pope's confectioner had unwittingly slipped his master the poison while making "a dish of chocolate".

4. The nasty marquis

The Marquis de Sade is one of history's vilest villains and biggest chocoholics. We get the word *sadist* (someone who delights in inflicting pain) from the name De Sade. Born in Paris in 1740, he wrote cruel stories which outraged all of Europe. He had plenty of time to write since he spent most of his life in prison.

The mad Marquis was nuts about chocolate. He devoured the sweet stuff in bucketfuls and once wrote to his wife from prison asking for a chocolate cake as black as the devil's bottom. He also asked for chocolate creams, chocolate pastilles, chocolate biscuits, etc.

Stuffing himself with chocolate made the Marquis as porky as a prize pig, but it did much worse things for his victims.

MONSIEUR DE SADE MAKES EXCEEDINGLY BAD CAKES!

According to report, cunning De Sade once gave a ball and served chocolate pastilles in the dessert. They were so delicious that they were gobbled up by the guests, who didn't suspect that they were laced with a powerful drug. After the ball many guests were sick as a dog – while a number actually died.

Naturally De Sade got the blame and fled to Sardinia where the king had him arrested and locked in a fortress prison. Back in France, Parliament sentenced him to death. The only snag was De Sade didn't hang around to take his punishment like a man, he escaped and went on the run. That didn't stop the French authorities: they executed a dummy in his place!

ANY LAST REQUESTS? A GOTTLE OF GEER!

5. The bishop who banned chocolate

Chocolate got up the nose of the seventeenth-century church in more ways than one. The Bishop of Chiapa in Mexico found that his cathedral services were being ruined by chocoholics. The noble ladies of that city were so hooked on chocolate that they couldn't last a church service without a refill of their favourite drink. (They claimed they had weak stomachs, poor lambs.) This meant that during the bishop's sermon, maids would continually be barging in and out of church, carrying cups of steaming chocolate to their mistresses.

Not surprisingly, the bishop got hot under the clerical collar. He put up a notice on the church door stating that anyone who ate or drank during his services would be excommunicated (slung out of the Catholic Church).

It was now the turn of the ladies of Chiapa to get steamed up. Many ignored the bishop's threat and continued sipping their favourite tipple in church. This simmering feud went on until one day swords were drawn against the priests who dared to try and seize the precious chocolate.

The war raged back and forth until finally the ladies of Chiapa struck the ultimate blow. Unwilling to leave the church or give up their chocolate, they found a simpler solution – poisoning the bishop! The dirty deed was done with a cup of chocolate. Rumour had it that a gentlewoman who was friendly with one of the bishop's pages persuaded him to slip the poison into his master's cup. The poisoner claimed afterwards that the bishop was such an enemy of chocolate that perhaps the drink hadn't agreed with his body. A proverb soon grew up in that country: "Beware of the chocolate of Chiapa!"

Nobbled nobles, poisoned guests, bumped-off bishops – the seventeenth century was littered with victims. So next time you hear someone say...

Be warned – THEY MAY BE SERIOUS!

Triffic trivia

1. Forget bacon and eggs, the English breakfast of the seventeenth century was chocolate or coffee served with rolls and eaten at leisure between nine and ten in the morning.

2. In 1701 chocolate was used to smuggle gold into the Spanish port of Cadiz. Port officials found eight crates of chocolate were suspiciously heavy. They turned out to be gold bars thinly coated in chocolate.

3. In 1807 Napoleon captured the city of Danzig. He gave the governor a dukedom and 100,000 ecus (coins) disguised as a bar of chocolate.

4. In 1764 Frederick the Great of Prussia commissioned one of his scientists to make chocolate from lime leaves. The recipe didn't catch on!

5. Prince Dietrichstein of Austria met his future wife in Vienna. She was the waitress who served him a cup of chocolate in a café. A portrait of "the chocolate girl" can still be seen today on Baker's chocolate in America.

6. During the eighteenth century chocolate was believed to purify the blood, improve sleep and help in the delivery of babies. None of these claims were true.

The fashionable French

"They presented next the Chocolate, each cup of porcelain on a saucer of agate garnished with gold... There was iced chocolate, another hot, and another with Milk and Eggs; one took it with a Biscuit or rather with dry small Buns."
Madame D'Aulnoy, French writer

The Spanish couldn't keep chocolate a secret for ever. No one knows for certain how the good news spread to France but it was certainly there by 1660 when Louis XIV of France married the Spanish princess, Maria Theresa.

Maria brought her own supply of chocolate and a maid to prepare her favourite drink. The French court nicknamed the maid La Molina after the chocolate-beating stick used at the time. Maria Theresa once declared: "Chocolate and the king are my only passions."

Notice that chocolate comes first and the king a poor second!

At first Maria sipped her chocolate in private, but within ten years the drink was all the rage at court. At the time, Louis XIV's court at the palace of Versailles was the splendour of Europe. 10,000 nobles and servants waited on the king's every wish at court. France was the fashion leader of Europe and so chocolate was in or out according to the latest fad. The letters of the French aristocrat, Madame de Sévigné, show how fast fashions could change.

11 February 1671, to her daughter

"You are not well, you have hardly slept, chocolate will set you up again. But you do not have a chocolatiere (chocolate-pot): I have thought of it a thousand times, what will you do?"

(Two months later) 15 April

"...chocolate is no longer for me what it was, fashion has led me astray as it always does. Everyone who spoke well of it now tells me bad things about it, it is cursed and accused of causing one's ills... In the name of God, don't keep it up."

25 October

"The Marquise de Coetlogon took so much chocolate during her pregnancy last year that she produced a small boy as black as the devil, who died."

(Three days later) **28 October**

"I have reconciled myself to chocolate, I took it the day before yesterday to digest my dinner and I took it yesterday to nourish me so that I could fast until evening: it gave me all the effects I wanted. That's what I like about it."

The café crazy English

What about the English? Last time we met them they were burning cocoa beans as sheep's droppings. But the English saw the light after 1657 when an advert appeared in the *Public Advertiser*.

ADVERT
Chocolate an excellent drink, sold in Queen's Head alley, in Bishopsgate St, by a Frenchman ...being the first man who did sell it in England. There you may have it ready to drink and also unmade at easie rates.

This humble advert (promoting the Spanish idea that chocolate was good for your health) was the start of England's continuing passion for chocolate.

In France, chocolate was the drink of kings and their courtiers, but in England it was available to anyone with coins jingling in their pocket. Soon chocolate and coffee houses sprung up all over London. It was the start of the café craze! Not that the cafés were much like the ones we're used to today. The drinks on the menu included coffee, tea and chocolate as well as sherbert (a sweet fruit drink) and cock ale – a beer in which you might find bits of boiled chicken swimming around.

The London chocolate houses soon became the favourite haunt of gentlemen of leisure. Fashionable cafés like White's, St James's, and The Smyrna were all within a short stroll of each other, so a dedicated chocoholic could visit them all in an hour. Inside, aristocrats and traders rubbed shoulders, drinking chocolate, gossiping and gambling. At White's you could buy tickets for shows of the day. If you wanted you could watch a panther fighting bulls and dogs fighting bears (bear-baiting). The point of this cruel sport was to bet on which animal would bite the dust first.

Gossiping in cafés soon became so popular that King Charles II tried to put a stop to it. He was worried that coffee and chocolate houses were hot beds of political unrest. The two great political parties of the day were the Tories and the Whigs – although it was sometimes hard to tell them apart.

TORY IN WIG

WHIG IN WIG

The Tories were loyal royalists but the Whigs didn't support the king. Charles (stupidly) thought if he could stop gossiping in chocolate and coffee houses then he would be safer on his throne. The law he passed in 1675 said:

> *It is forbidden to keep any public Coffee House, or sell by retail ... any Coffee, Chocolate, Sherbet or Tea.*

Did it close down the chocolate houses? Not likely! Englishmen weren't going to give up their coffee or chocolate just for a right Charlie even if he was the king! They went on drinking and gossiping just the same and the law was eventually forgotten.

Diary of a chocoholic

Luckily, one of the celebrated chocoholics of the day kept a detailed diary. Samuel Pepys's diary is one of the most famous in history because:

a) it gives us a wonderful picture of seventeenth-century England;

b) it dishes the dirt on people that Pepys knew. Here are a few snippets which show you Pepys's dedicated pursuit of chocolate:

• Samuel Pepys's Diary

1660   When I came home I found a Quantity of Chocolate left for me, but I know not from whom.

24 April 1661   (following the coronation of Charles II)   Waked in the morning with my head in a sad taking through the last night's drink, which I am very sorry for; so rose and went with Mr Creed to drink our morning draught, which he did give me in Chocolate to settle my stomach.

26 February 1664   Up and after dressing myself handsomely for riding, I out and by water to Westminster to Mr Creed's chamber, and after drinking some Chocolatte and playing on the vyall...

3 May 1664   Up and being ready, went by agreement to Mr Bland's and there drank my morning draught in good Chocolatte, and slabbering my band [dribbling down my necktie] sent home for another.

(In the diary Pepys writes either chocolatte, jocolatte or chocolate. Spelling obviously wasn't a passion like chocolate.)

Almost a century later the chocolate houses that Pepys would have visited at White's and St James's were still around. But by then they had become dens of gambling where the customers included villains of every type.

> "Dissipated and broken captains, sharpers, and even highwaymen of the more presentable type were constantly to be met at the Chocolate House; judges there were liable to meet the man whom they might afterwards have to sentence in the dock; it was no uncommon thing in those days to recognise a body swinging in chains on a heath outside London as man whom you had called a main at hazard [a cheat at cards] a few weeks before at White's or at the Cocoa tree."
>
> *Amusements of London*

One of the gaming rooms at White's was simply called Hell. Customers would bet fortunes of money on absolutely anything. Here are two true tales of bets that were made at White's by bored gentlemen.

'A RAINY DAY AT WHITE'S'

So how did the seventeenth-century English gentleman drink his chocolate? Not for him the hours of beating and the complicated recipes of the Spanish. The English wanted their chocolate and they wanted it in a hurry! A chocolate recipe of the day recommends that you...

Take a cake of chocolate, pounding it in a mortar or grate it into fine powder. Mix this with sugar and pour it into a little pot in which water is boiling. Then, take the pot from the fire and work it well with your little Mill; if you don't have a mill, pour it a score (twenty) of times from one pot to another, but this is not as good. Finally, let it be drunk without separating the scum from it.

Slaving for chocolate

While the English gentleman sipped his chocolate did he ever spare a thought for the lives of the slaves who provided him with cocoa beans? Workers were often African slaves taken to the West Indies as part of the slave triangle between Britain, West Africa and the Caribbean.

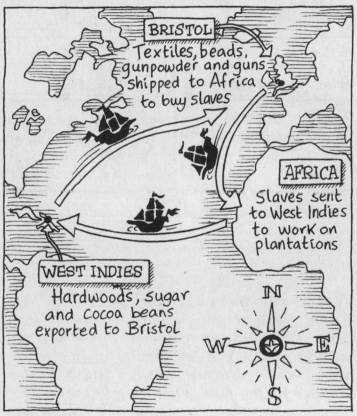

BRISTOL
Textiles, beads, gunpowder and guns shipped to Africa to buy slaves

AFRICA
Slaves sent to West Indies to work on plantations

WEST INDIES
Hardwoods, sugar and cocoa beans exported to Bristol

The triangle made many slave traders rich, but life on a cocoa plantation for the slaves was short and not at all sweet.

THE JOURNEY TO THE WEST INDIES OR THE AMERICAS TOOK 6-9 WEEKS. MANY SLAVES DIED ON THE WAY 	SLAVES WHO SURVIVED WORKED FOR NOTHING ON THE PLANTATIONS 
A NORMAL WORKING DAY WAS 18-20 HOURS LONG 	A "DRIVER" WHIPPED THE SLAVES TO WORK HARDER 

Slavery wasn't abolished in Britain and its colonies until 1833. By then it was too late for the millions who had died of illness or overwork on the plantations.

Weird recipe: chicken mole

It's OK. Mexican mole sauce doesn't contain any of those sweet little black creatures who live underground. It's a chocolate sauce, said to have been invented by the nuns of Santa Rosa in Mexico. The Aztecs were also keen on topping their meat with chocolate sauce. So if it was good enough for Montezuma...

THAT'S A RELIEF!

Ingredients
chicken breasts
garlic
1 medium-sized onion – sliced
small tortilla cut into strips
30 g of raisins
30 g of blanched almonds
1 tablespoon sesame seeds
2 tablespoons olive oil
7 teaspoons mild chilli powder
quarter of a teaspoon each of: cumin, cloves, cinnamon, coriander seeds, anise, sugar
25 g unsweetened chocolate – melted
700 ml chicken broth
250 g tomatoes

Method:
1. Brown the chicken on all sides in some hot oil.
2. Blend the next seven ingredients to make a smooth paste.

3. Add the chilli powder, seasonings and melted chocolate.
4. Heat the olive oil in a frying pan and fry the sauce for five minutes, lowering the heat and stirring to prevent burning.
5. Stir in the broth and add the chicken. Cover and simmer over a low heat for 30 minutes or until tender.
6. Invite your friends to supper and watch their faces when you announce you're eating mole.

Throughout the seventeenth and eighteenth centuries chocolate still remained a heavy, fatty drink. Although chocolate cakes and rolls made an appearance, no one had yet dreamed of sweets made of solid yummy chocolate.

Chocolate arrived in America in 1765 with an Irish immigrant called John Hannon, who persuaded his partner, Dr James Baker, to set up a chocolate factory. Unfortunately for Hannon he was drowned twelve years later on his way to buy cocoa beans in the West Indies. Baker was left and you can still buy his chocolate in America today.

In England the royal doctor, Sir Hans Sloane, was the first to have the brainwave of mixing milk with chocolate instead of water. This idea would later catch on with two English brothers called Cadbury. But for them and the other great heroes of chocolate history, we must wait till the next chapter.

Heroes of Chocolate – The Nineteenth Century

1800–1900 The sticky age of discovery

1807 The slave trade is finally abolished in the British Empire. Good news for cocoa workers.

1819 Francois-Louis Cailler opens the first Swiss chocolate factory on Lake Geneva.

1824 John Cadbury opens his shop in Birmingham to sell tea, coffee and cocoa.

1828 Dutchman Van Houten invents a way to take the fat out of cocoa beans.

1847 Joseph Fry of Bristol invents the first chocolate bar – but it will take another 50 years to catch on.

1850 British enquiry finds brick dust in chocolate.

1853 Tax on chocolate is fixed at a penny a pound in England. Chocolate is no longer just for the rich.

1862 Henry Rowntree starts up his cocoa and chocolate business in York.

1866 Cadbury launch cocoa essence – pure cocoa without the added brick dust!

1866 Fry's Chocolate Cream bar hits the shops and stays around for the next 130 years!

1868 The first box of chocs is sold by Richard Cadbury with his own painting featured on the lid.

1870 Amazingly, chocolate is still hardly known in America.

1876 Daniel Peter in Switzerland experiments with condensed milk supplied by Henri Nestlé. The world's first milk chocolate is born!

1879 Cadbury start their "factory and village in a garden" in Bournville, Birmingham. Workers are taken out of the slums and into the country.

1880 Swiss chocolate-maker Rodolphe Lindt, leaves a batch to mix for

several days and discovers "melt in the mouth" chocolate.

1900 American Milton Hershey decides "caramels are a fad, chocolate is a permanent thing". He builds his chocolate town, Hershey, in Pennsylvania.

Since its first discovery chocolate had been a drink enjoyed only by the bigwigs in society. Even in the nineteenth century cocoa would be promoted as a drink for *real men*. Hunters, soldiers and firemen were the sort of rough, tough, manly chaps who'd enjoy drinking cocoa. That great detective, Sherlock Holmes, always took a cup for breakfast before going out to solve another grisly murder in Victorian London.

But things were about to change. The nineteenth century was the era of the heroes of chocolate. These were the great pioneers in Switzerland, Great

Britain and America who made chocolate what it is today – not a drink for the rich or manly, but a sweet yummy food for everyone.

If it wasn't for the heroes of chocolate, we might still be drinking cups of scummy stuff like the Aztecs and wishing we had something more solid to nibble on. There are many names in the book of chocolate heroes – some of them, like Cadbury, Mars and Nestlé, you'll know. Others, like Daniel Peter of Switzerland, probably haven't had the credit they deserve. But the grandad of them all – the patron saint of chocolate – was a Dutchman called Van Houten.

Heroes of chocolate

No. 1: Van Houten, the low-fat Dutchman

Coenraad Van Houten was a chemist in Holland. In his Amsterdam factory he was wrestling with a fatty problem. Not that he was overweight: it was the chocolate. Remember it often had a nasty scum on the surface? That was the fat or cocoa butter – a natural part of the cacao bean. To absorb the fat, people put flour or cornmeal into their chocolate (and sometimes more revolting things which we'll meet later). Yet despite every effort chocolate remained a fatty drink – until Van Houten got to work.

Van Houten's invention was a press to squeeze the fat out of the chocolate liquor.

In one stroke Van Houten reduced the amount of fat in chocolate by a half. What was left was a fine brown powder – cocoa!

Van Houten's press paved the way for the invention of eating chocolate. It appeared in 1828 and was soon snapped up by other chocolate makers like Cadbury and Fry in England.

The smart Swiss

Think of Switzerland and you think of mountains, skiing and, of course, chocolate. Companies like Lindt and Suchard-Tobler (who make triangular Toblerone) produce some of the most famous chocolate in the world.

But Switzerland wasn't always keen on the sticky stuff. It was only due to the efforts of a few dedicated heroes that Swiss products leapt to the top of the chocs during the nineteenth and twentieth centuries. The Swiss pioneers cashed in on one thing their country had a lot of.

Heroes of chocolate

No. 2: Francois-Louis Cailler (1796–1852)

As the first to open a factory, Cailler is the grandaddy of Swiss chocolate. It all started at a local fair where young Francois's nostrils were tickled by the most delectable whiff he'd ever come across. Following the smell, he found Italian chocolate-makers stirring a pot of dark, sticky liquid. One taste and Francois was hooked for life. He threw a spare pair of long johns into a bag and took off to Milan in Italy where he worked for four years in the Caffarel chocolate factory.

By the time he returned home, Cailler was a master chocolate-maker. In 1819 he opened his first factory on Lake Geneva. Swiss chocolate was up and running.

No. 3: Phillippe Suchard (1797–1884)

Phillippe Suchard's name still appears on fine Swiss chocolate today. He was only 12 years old when he caught the chocolate bug. On that fateful day, young Phil was sent to the chemist's to collect a pound of chocolate for his sick mother. The cost of the chocolate was enough to make anyone sick. It was a whopping six francs – three days' wages for a worker in those days! Phillippe started to think – if chocolate cost that much then there must be a shortage of the stuff. And if there was a shortage then somebody needed to start making more.

By 1826, he'd begun making his own chocolate using machinery he'd invented himself.

Nos. 4 and 5: Henri Nestlé (1814–90) and Daniel Peter (1836–1919)

Everyone knows the name of Nestlé. Today Kit Kat and Milky Bar are just two of the famous chocolate bars made by the world's largest food company. But Henri Nestlé didn't start out as a chocolate-maker – his story started with the Swiss secret weapon we mentioned before. Yes, Nestlé was a milk man. Not that he delivered pintas to the doorsteps of Swiss chalets, Nestlé's great invention was powdered milk. It could be fed to babies and children (mixed with water). What Nestlé didn't know was that his powdered milk could also be put to another use. For that he needed the help of a younger man – Daniel Peter. If we could see Daniel's diary we'd find he fell into the chocolate business almost by accident.

Diary of a milk chocolate maker

1851 Quel chance! Have landed a job in a grocer's shop. Madame Clement, my employer, also makes candles as a sideline. I see a great future in candles. I'll be rich beyond my wildest dreams. After all, can you imagine a time when candles won't be needed to light people to bed?

the future!

1852 I can't believe my luck, Madame Clement has handed the candle-making business over to me. Today she said to me, "Daniel, you're a clever boy and I can see you're up to your ears in wax already. Take on the candle-making business, it's starting to get on my wick." It's my big chance and I don't intend to let it slip.

1856 Mon Dieu! Today I saw a new invention selling in Geneva. They call it the paraffin lamp. You can light it whenever you want and it doesn't burn down and need replacing like a candle. In an instant all my hopes were snuffed out. The candle is doomed. Just think, one day people may only use them to decorate birthday cakes!

1857 I'm in love! My sweetheart is a wonderful girl called Fanny Cailler. What's more her father is a chocolate-maker. [Remember Francois-Louis Cailler?] I have tasted this sweet brown stuff. It's just as gloriously messy as candle-making only the smell doesn't get up my nose so much. I have decided to throw myself into chocolate to learn its secrets.

CHOCOLATE ← Me throwing myself in

1875 Eureka! I've done it! After years of experiments I have succeeded in blending milk powder with chocolate. The result I call milk chocolate. I wonder if it will ever catch on?

RESULT! →

MILK CHOC

INK

The rest, as they say, is history. Daniel Peter deserves the world's undying gratitude for discovering creamy milk chocolate which millions enjoy today. He went on to create the world's first milk chocolate bar. So it's lucky for us that the paraffin lamp came along at the right time.

Daniel Peter was the hero of milk chocolate, but what about the maker of the world's first chocolate bar? Twenty-four years before Peter's invention it was done by an Englishman...

The quaking English

The English heroes of chocolate are all Quakers. Quakers, or the Society of Friends, started in the seventeenth century as a breakaway religious movement from the Church of England. Why were they known as Quakers? Because early members were said to tremble and quake when they were filled with the Spirit of God.

By the nineteenth century quaking had largely disappeared from the movement but what was left was a strong belief in justice, peace and an end to poverty. Why did they go into the chocolate business? For one thing their choices were limited. As outsiders who didn't belong to the Established Church they were barred from going to university, entering law, medicine or politics. They couldn't join the army or navy since they were pacifists who didn't agree with war.

That left business and industry. One Quaker called Lloyd founded a bank (heard of Lloyd's bank?), several others, including Cadbury, Fry and Rowntree, became great heroes of chocolate. Originally they chose to make cocoa because they saw it as a healthy alternative to the demon drink (alcohol). They hoped to persuade the poor to give up gin and beer and drink cocoa instead. This, said the Quakers, would be much better for their health.

Heroes of chocolate
No. 6: Joseph Fry (1728–87)

You've probably heard of Fry's Chocolate Cream or Fry's Turkish Delight. The original firm of JS Fry and Sons was formed over 200 ago by Dr Joseph Fry in Bristol. Up to the mid-nineteenth century the only chocolate you could eat was dry, brittle pastilles and cakes made in France. In 1847 the Fry firm experimented with mixing a blend of cocoa powder and sugar with melted cocoa butter. The result was chocolate which could be moulded into a shape. At a stroke Fry had created the world's first real chocolate bar. The choc bar went on display at an exhibition in Birmingham in 1849. Fry called it:

Chocolat Delicieux a Manger

(French was considered fashionably posh in those days.) For a long time eating chocolate would remain too expensive for ordinary people, but that would change by the turn of the century.

No. 7: Henry Isaac Rowntree (around 1837–1883)

Henry Rowntree got into the chocolate business by marriage – taking over the business from his father-in-law, William Tuke. At the start he was a step behind his two great rivals – Cadbury and Fry. First, the company's policy didn't allow him to advertise and, second, he didn't have the cash to buy a Van Houten press. As a result, Rowntree's cocoa still contained fatty cocoa butter. But Henry was a clever chap and made up for it by dreaming up lots of silly names for his cocoa. These names were in fact based on the many different things he was chucking into his cocoa powder to take away the taste of the horrible fat!

Don't drink the cocoa!

You might think Rowntree was making a mistake in boasting that his cocoa wasn't pure, but what he was adding was mild compared to some of his rivals. During the Victorian era adding foul ingredients to cocoa was common and the practice also flourished in Europe and America.

Have a look at the list of foul ingredients below. Can you guess which ones were added to cocoa?

Answer:
All of these were at some time added to cocoa during the nineteenth century! Red lead and vermilion are actually *poisons* so it's best if you steer clear of them. The others probably tasted pretty foul too. In 1850 the British government set up a health commission to investigate complaints about cocoa and other food products being corrupted. Out of 70 samples of drinking chocolate they found that 39 had been coloured with red brick dust! If that wasn't bad enough, *all* the samples contained potato starch. Not surprisingly, laws were passed in 1860 and 1872 to try and stamp out this foul practice.

Heroes of chocolate

No. 8: John Cadbury (1801–89)

Cadbury – one of the most famous names in British chocolate – started from a single shop in Birmingham. John Cadbury sold mainly tea and coffee but his customers soon developed a taste for the cocoa he advertised in the *Birmingham Gazette*:

John Cadbury is desirous of introducing to particular notice COCOA NIBS prepared by himself, an article affording a most nutritious beverage for breakfast

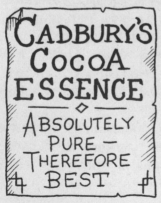

CADBURY'S COCOA ESSENCE — ◇ — ABSOLUTELY PURE — THEREFORE BEST

Cadbury's sons, Richard and George, took over the business in 1861 and within five years had bought a Van Houten press. Having de-fatted their cocoa, they launched an effective advertising campaign.

It was a clever way of saying their cocoa didn't contain brick dust, iron filings or other foul ingredients. Their competitors were shocked at such a scandalous suggestion (never mind if it was true), but Cadbury's Cocoa Essence was an instant hit with the public. Fry's fought back with their own fat-free, "Cocoa Extract". But two years later, in 1868, the Cadbury brothers brought out the first box of chocolates:

The chocolates weren't much like the ones you get in a box today. They were mostly sweet, candy-covered chocolates. But the box had a picture painted by Richard Cadbury of his daughter, Jessica, holding a kitten. The Victorians loved cute pictures of kiddies so it helped to sell a lot of chocolates.

Slummy cities

Quakers like the Cadburys tried to look after their workers but for many Victorian factory workers life was no picnic.

Most cities and towns in Victorian Britain had slum areas where the poor workers lived. After a long day at the factory this is what you'd come home to:

BACK TO BACK HOUSES — NO BATHROOMS, NO GARDENS — POTTIES EMPTIED STRAIGHT INTO THE GUTTERS

OY!

STREETS SOGGY AND BOGGY

Young children died fast in these damp, stinking hovels. As one Birmingham slum-dweller put it:

THERE'S MORE BUGS THAN BABIES

As Quakers, it bothered the Cadbury brothers that their factory workers had to live like pigs (in fact most pigs were better off). George Cadbury gave it a lot of thought and, at last, hit on a solution.

Why should not the industrial worker enjoy country air and occupations without being separated from his work? If the country is a good place to live in, why not to work in?
George Cadbury

WATER CART SELLING DIRTY WATER TO DRINK

SMOKY FACTORIES

KNACKER & CO SLAUGHTERERS

STINKY SLAUGHTERHOUSES

In 1879 the Cadbury brothers bought a 15-acre site and moved their factory out to the country four miles south of Birmingham. They built a whole village for workers and called it Bournville. (Fashionable French again. Ville means town, Bourn was a local stream. Hence Bournville.) The houses were a big improvement on the slums of the city. They were cottages on tree-lined streets, each with a front garden and a vegetable patch. In those days gardens were unheard of for poor workers. Later, the houses even had the fabulous luxury of their own bathroom!

The Cadbury brothers didn't stop there. They wanted their factory workers to be healthy and happy. There were no pubs in Bournville because of the Cadburys' religious beliefs, but there were parks and gardens, swimming pools (equipped with the latest hair dryers), football pitches, concert halls and works outings into the country. All that and the smell of chocolate all week.

A day in the life of a Cadbury's worker (1930)

8 a.m. Arrive at the factory and clock in for work. Prizes given for punctuality. Down to work putting Cadbury's Dairy Milk in moulds. Men and women aren't allowed to mix so that they keep their minds on the job!

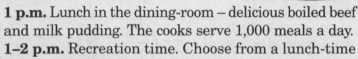

10.30 a.m. Tea break

1 p.m. Lunch in the dining-room – delicious boiled beef and milk pudding. The cooks serve 1,000 meals a day.

1–2 p.m. Recreation time. Choose from a lunch-time concert, a walk in the gardens or a session under the sun-lamp to stop you catching a cold.

2–6 p.m. Back to work in the factory. Hand-dipping chocolates.

3 p.m. Tea break. Anyone for a chocolate biscuit?

4 p.m. Sit on one of our workers' committees. Our task is to taste new products and report back. It's a tough job but someone's got to do it!

6 p.m. The horn goes for home time. Join the sea of bicycles pouring out of the gates.

6.15 p.m. Works football match, Cadbury v. Rowntree. (Lost 2–1. Boo!)

8 p.m. A quick dip in the men's swimming-baths.

9 p.m. Home in ten minutes for bed and a nice cup of cocoa (Cadbury's, of course).

Queen Vic's chocolate soldiers

In 1900, when eating chocolate was just beginning to catch on, Britain was fighting the Boer War against Dutch settlers in South Africa. (This was the second Boer war so it was all getting a bit boering.) Queen Victoria was outraged when she heard that British officers in the war were doing much better for gifts sent from home than the ordinary soldiers. She decided to send her own royal New Year's gift and what better than the popular new treat called chocolate?

Cadbury were asked to produce the royal choccie. It was an honour, but put the Cadbury brothers in a real fix. As pacifists they didn't approve of war, so they didn't want to supply the British army. On the other hand, if they said "nuts" to the Queen they'd risk making themselves pretty unpopular (especially with her royal high and mightiness). What do you think they did?

a) Took the order?

b) Invited their rivals to share the order with them?

c) Turned it down and went into hiding?

Answer: b)

The Cadbury brothers cleverly invited Rowntree and Fry to share the order with them. That way they figured none of their rivals could point a finger at them for abandoning their anti-war beliefs. The tin – with Queen Vic's head on the lid – was designed by Fry, who took care to keep their name off the lid.

The plan was for the chocolate to bear no maker's name either. But Victoria soon scotched that idea. She didn't want her soldiers to think she was sending them any old brand of chocolate. Of the big three companies it was finally Cadbury's name that appeared on the bar.

The chocolate was received with delight by the hungry troops in South Africa (hardly surprising since some of them had been reduced to eating horse-meat). The nice tin boxes came in handy too – when a soldier died in battle, the box was sent home to his wife along with the dead man's things.

HE MIGHT HAVE LEFT ME SOME CHOCOLATE!

"Pass the chocolate, Jeeves"

In Victorian and Edwardian times servants were given strict advice about chocolate etiquette. If you were a butler or a maid there was a lot to remember.

1. The servant should indicate discreetly if a gentleman guest should get froth or cream attached to his moustache or beard while drinking cocoa.

2. Should the young gentleman return to the house after taking exercise, allow him time to perform his ablutions and cool down before presenting him with a nourishing cup of cocoa.

3. Take care not to put a box of chocolates in a clothes drawer containing moth balls. The odour will spoil the taste.
4. If the maid sees that the evening is drawing to an early close because of lack of enthusiasm, she would do well to suggest the lady of the house offer a selection of eating chocolate to revive her guests.

> 5. The nursery maid must keep a close eye on children when eating-chocolates are offered to the company. Children must be prevented from grabbing greedily and instructed to offer the chocolates to guests first.
>
> ALL RIGHT! ALL RIGHT! I'LL OFFER THEM TO THE GUESTS!
>
> CHOC

(Taken from *Etiquette for Chocolate Lovers* by Beryl Peters.)

The automated Americans

Americans were late in getting the taste for chocolate but they've made up for it ever since. Chocolate was introduced to the USA in 1765 by John Hannon and Dr James Baker. (You can still buy Baker's chocolate today.) But until the end of the nineteenth century it was known only as a drink. One man changed all that.

Heroes of chocolate

No. 9: Milton Hershey (1857–1945)

Milton Snavely Hershey was a man who thought *big*. He has been called "the Henry Ford of chocolate-makers". As Henry Ford introduced machines and mass production to the motor car, Hershey did the same for chocolate.

FORD'S MOTOR CAR

HERSHEY'S CHOCOLATE BAR

HERSHEY MILK CHOCOLATE

When you think about it, Hershey was the greater of the two pioneers. After all, when did a bar of chocolate ever choke the air with poisonous fumes?

Making the first mass-produced chocolate wasn't Hershey's only claim to fame. He also built his own wacky chocolate town (named Hershey, of course).

At the age of 15, Hershey started out as a humble apprentice in a sweet factory. Four years later the whizz-kid of sweets had his own candy business. Caramels were his bag, but he saw the light in 1893 when he visited an exhibition and saw a machine making chocolate. Hershey knew at once he had seen the future and bought the machine on the spot.

Back home, he sold off his caramel business for a cool million dollars and started to build his chocolate factory in Pennsylvania. Everything was done by machines and conveyor belts so that he could soon turn out his bite-size "Hershey's Kisses" by the thousand.

Once he had his factory, Hershey set to work on his model town. It was like the Cadbury brothers' Bournville, only naturally much, much *bigger*. In Hershey there are streets named Chocolate or Cocoa Avenue and even the lamps are shaped like Hershey's Kisses.

MILK CHOCOLATE AND COCOA FACTORY

HERSHEY DEPT. STORE

SCHOOL FOR ORPHANS

HERSHEY PARK AND GARDENS

COCOA AVE

CHOCOLATE AVE

KISS-SHAPED STREET LAMPS

Milton Hershey died peacefully aged 85 but his chocolate empire lives on. You can still go to Hershey in Pennsylvania and be taken round the Disneyland of chocolate. And Hershey's Kisses are still as popular as ever – over 25 million a day came off the conveyor belt in the 1990s. Europeans are still baffled by the Americans' love of the Hershey bar. "Who in their right minds would produce such a sour chocolate?" asked one Swiss chocolatier. Some claim that the milk that Hershey used in his original recipe had gone sour but he was too tight-fisted to throw it away. Naturally the Hershey company denies this unwholesome story. They say that Americans just happen to like the unique flavour of their choccie. Meanwhile Europeans go on turning up their noses.

School for chocolate

Van Houten, Suchard, Peter, Fry, Cadbury, Hershey ... the roll call of the heroes of chocolate is a proud one. But these are important names you should learn about at school. What are teachers thinking of? Never mind William the Conqueror and Henry VIII, just think: if it wasn't for Daniel Peter we might never have tasted the smooth creamy taste of milk chocolate!

"If I were a headmaster, I would get rid of the history teacher and get a chocolate teacher instead."

Roald Dahl, best-selling author of *Charlie and the Chocolate Factory*.

The nineteenth century saw a huge leap forward in the story of chocolate. Instead of the fatty drink that people had put up with for centuries, chocolate was changed into the triffic sweet we know today. But that wasn't the end of the story, the best was yet to come in the twentieth century. The next 40 years were the golden age of chocolate when names like Mars, Milky Way, Crunchie and Kit Kat would change our lives for ever.

The golden age

1905 Cadbury's Dairy Milk is launched – and remains the queen of British moulded chocolate today.

1907 Hershey's Kisses are invented and America takes them to its heart.

1908 Toblerone is born. The triangular shape is inspired by Swiss mountains.

1910 The dark one, Cadbury's Bournville joins its paler sister.

1915 Cadbury's Milk Tray is a soft-centred hit.

1920 The first speciality bar hits the shops – the Cadbury's Flake. Inventors start to play with new shapes, textures and ingredients.

1921 Cadbury go nutty with the Fruit and Nut Bar.

1930 The classic age of the choc bar – the 1930s kick off with Fry's invention of the Crunchie. Unfortunately, at

first it's more like the Crumbly.

1932 The Mars bar is invented by American, Forrest Mars. The chew bar is a smash hit with Brits selling two million in its first year.

1933 Black Magic appears in boxes and is a best-seller. Market research hints at questioning guests at a royal garden party.

1935 Aero, the bar with the tiny bubbles, bursts on the scene and is instantly popular.

1936 Forrest Mars experiments with exploding a pea-sized pellet of dough in a vacuum. He coats the result with chocolate. The Malteser is born.

1937 A bumper year for chocolate. Kit Kat, Rolos and Smarties all make their entry.

1940 The US army recognizes the importance of chocolate by asking Hershey to invent a chocolate bar that can survive hot climates in a soldier's pocket. It's imaginatively called...

92

1970s Modern choccie bars come thick and fast. Cadbury's Double Decker is one of the success stories, selling 160 million in its first year.

1996 Cadbury's see a gap in the market for a "substantial snack". In its first year Fuse becomes the second best-selling choc bar behind the mighty Kit Kat.

Fry were the ones to start it all in Britain. For 50 years they'd been trying to come up with chocolate to challenge the Swiss and French. Early experiments were too bitter and crumbly. But in 1902 they brought out the Five Boys bar – their best yet. Cadbury took up the challenge and three years later brought out Cadbury's Dairy Milk. It was to become one of the all time greats – the queen of British moulded chocolate. (That's chocolate set in a mould, unlike mouldy chocolate which is choccie that's been left too long.)

What followed in the twentieth century was a chocolate explosion. Every great invention has its golden age and for the choccie bar it was the 1930s. During that decade many of the great names in chocolate burst on the world. Before the 1930s sweet shops were just that. They sold sweets rather than chocolates. If you turned out a child's pockets in the 1920s this is what you'd have found.

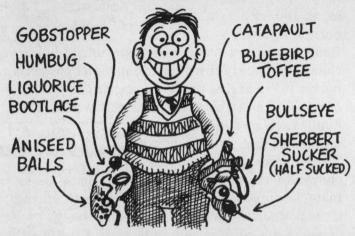

GOBSTOPPER
HUMBUG
LIQUORICE
BOOTLACE
ANISEED
BALLS

CATAPAULT
BLUEBIRD
TOFFEE
BULLSEYE
SHERBERT
SUCKER
(HALF SUCKED)

It didn't worry kids in those days that liquorice was made from rat's blood or sherbet from sawdust. (Yes, really – according to author Roald Dahl.) Sweets were what they wanted. Chocolate was still expensive and didn't offer the same Aladdin's cave of choice. In 1920 you had just two choices – milk chocolate (such as Dairy Milk) or plain (Bournville). Chocolate bars with 50 different chewy centres of toffee, caramel, peanuts or raisins were undreamt of. Then came the 1930s and the chocolate revolution. Many of the great classics born in this era – such as the Mars bar, Milky Way, Crunchie and Aero – are still with us today. But who dreamt them up and how did they get their names?

Our top ten guide will tell you everything you want to know about your favourite choc bars.

Top of the chocs: ten of the best

1. Cadbury's Dairy Milk

Born: 1905
Parent: Cadbury

Cadbury's Dairy Milk nearly started life as a bar called Highland Milk. That was one of the original names planned just weeks before Cadbury's bar was due to hit the streets. In the end two names, Dairy Maid and Highland Milk, were merged to give us Dairy Milk. The big difference from other chocolate was the creamy taste – using real milk rather than powdered stuff. The first Dairy Milk was sold as a half-pound cake and cost sixpence.

WELL, I THINK IT SHOULD HAVE BEEN CALLED HIGHLAND MAID!

Sales of Dairy Milk have grown nearly every year since the bar's launch. The Russians love the bar even more than the British – in 1995 they wolfed down 280 million of them!

Did you know? In 1905, when Dairy Milk first appeared, King Edward VII sat on the throne and you could buy tea for 1s and 6d a pound (about 7p) or travel to America third class on a steamer for just £6.

2. Milky Way

Born: 1923
Parent: Mars

In 1923 Frank Mars and his son, Forrest, were sitting in a milk bar drinking chocolate milk shakes.

Frank was a sweet-maker but he had a problem; his sweets didn't stay fresh long enough to be sold outside his home state of Minnesota. He asked his son what he should do.

"Why don't you put this chocolate malted drink in a candy bar," was Forrest's off-hand reply.

Later he explained: "I was just saying anything that entered my head. And I'll be damned if a short time afterwards, he has a candy bar. And it's a chocolate malted drink. He put some caramel on top of it, and some chocolate around it – not very good chocolate, he was buying cheap chocolate – but that damn thing sold."

That damn thing was a Milky Way and we're still eating the milk shake in a bar today.

Did you know? Milky Way might have been Milky Day or even Milky Wave. Both names were registered by Mars so that competitors couldn't use them.

3. Mars Bar

Born: 1932

Parent: Mars

By 1932 young Forrest Mars had fallen out with his dad. Clutching the recipe for Milky Way in his sticky hand, along with $50,000, he left for England.

Young Forrest started in a small rented factory in Slough. But he wasn't content with producing his

96

pa's Milky Ways. So he altered them to suit English tastes, adding more sugar and sweeter caramel. Before you could say sweet heaven he'd invented the Mars bar!

With just a dozen staff making them by hand, Forrest sold them as two-penny bars. In 1933 block choccie was about all you could buy, so the chewy, gooey Mars bar caused a sensation. By the end of the first year Forrest employed 100 workers and he'd sold 2 million bars. Today 2.7 million bars are eaten in Britain every day! (Despite his success, Forrest wasn't so much a hero of chocolate as a monster from Mars! Read about him later.)

Did you know? It's not only humans who have lapped up Mars bars. In 1979 a racehorse called "No Bombs" won at Ascot by a canter. But a routine drug test revealed the nag had taken a banned substance called theobromine. It turned out "No Bombs" had swiped a Mars bar from his stable boy on the way to the races! The horse's trainer complained:

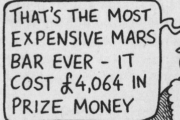

THAT'S THE MOST EXPENSIVE MARS BAR EVER - IT COST £4,064 IN PRIZE MONEY

4. Crunchie

Born: 1930
Parent: Fry
Appearance: Chocolate-covered honeycomb that packs a crunch.

In the world before Crunchie, children bought cinder toffee − big nuggets of crispy honeycomb − loose in bags. Then someone at Fry had the bright idea of wrapping the honeycomb in chocolate to create a new bar. At least it seemed like a bright idea at the time. First versions of the Crunchie should have been called "Crumbly" or even "Softie". They were so fragile, girls at Fry's factory had to use a blowtorch to weld broken bars together! Worse still, if the tiniest pinhole of air got in, the crunchy honeycomb centre collapsed. Result? The Crunchie was as soft as chewing gum.

Fry had to think of a solution before the Crunchie sunk as fast as the *Titanic*. A double coating of chocolate did the trick and the Crunchie survived its sticky start

Did you know? Fry turned their near disaster into an advertising slogan. "Crunchie − twice covered in chocolate!"

5. Kit Kat

Born: 1937
Parent: Rowntree

If the Mars bar was a winner, the Kit Kat was the chocolate champion of the 1990s. It has consistently sat at the top of the chocs as the best-seller of recent times (13 billion in 1995).

So what is it about Kit Kats? No peanuts, fudge, toffee or raisins to tempt our taste buds, just two or four wafers encased in smooth milk choccie. Maybe it's the lightness that kids us it's just a light snack so we don't need to feel guilty.

The Kit Kat recipe hasn't changed much since 1935 when it was first launched as Chocolate Crisp. That wasn't too catchy, so in 1937 the bar was rechristened with a new name borrowed from the eighteenth century London Kit Kat club.

During the Second World War Kit Kats were covered in dark chocolate because of a milk shortage. There has also been a mint Kit Kat and an orange-flavoured Kit Kat which sold three times as fast as the original. Chocoholics thrive on novelty, say the makers, but they turned down customers' suggestions to make liquorice, passion fruit or marshmallow Kit Kats. A pity really – but if you go to Japan you can buy a toasted almond Kit Kat and we now have the chunky Kit Kat – one finger but twice as fat.

Did you know? Every five minutes, enough Kit Kats are made to be piled higher than the Eiffel Tower. A year's production would stretch round London's Underground system more than 350 times.

6. Smarties

Born: 1937
Parent: Rowntree

Spare a thought for the light brown Smartie. In 1937 when the bright chocolate buttons were launched, the brown was there in the tube with its sisters – the red, yellow, orange, green, mauve, pink and dark brown. But in modern times, it came under threat from a flashy European rival. The Germans had come up with the blue Smartie, which soon marched into France, Italy, Belgium and Holland.

The British steadfastly stuck by the light brown which had seen them through a World War. But for the Smarties' 50th birthday bash in 1987 Nestlé-Rowntree announced the arrival of the blue Smartie. The light brown knew its dull days were numbered and sure enough, it was killed off two years later to make room for the new bean on the block. Sadly, the brown Smartie never lived to see the millennium.

Did you know? Every minute 16,000 Smarties disappear into hungry mouths.

7. Maltesers

Born: 1936
Parent: Mars
Appearance: Light malted-milk ball covered in thick chocolate.

Not content with having the Milky Way, the Snickers and the Mars bar, Forrest Mars went on experimenting with what he could do with chocolate.

The recipe for Maltesers was a surprising one.

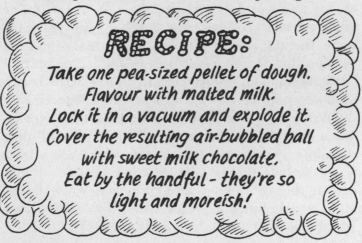

RECIPE:
Take one pea-sized pellet of dough.
Flavour with malted milk.
Lock it in a vacuum and explode it.
Cover the resulting air-bubbled ball
with sweet milk chocolate.
Eat by the handful – they're so
light and moreish!

Where did Mars get the brilliant idea for the Malteser? In a word he copied it, from another American sweet called Whoppers.

Did you know? Originally Maltesers were launched as "Energy balls", but somehow that made the British giggle. (For a similar reason Snickers bars used to be known as "Marathon bars" in Britain. The reason? Mr Mars thought the British would rhyme Snickers with "knickers" and get an attack of the sniggers.)

8. Yorkie

Born: 1976
Parent: Rowntree
Appearance: Milk chocolate bar that's a big, chunky mouthful.

For years the elegant Dairy Milk had things all its own way in the world of moulded milk chocolate. Then along came the big, barrel-chested Yorkie. Rowntree's old rival Cadbury had just reduced the thickness of the Dairy Milk because of a rise in cocoa prices. Rowntree saw their chance and launched a thick bar that looked like a chew bar, but was in fact slabs of solid milk chocolate. Yorkie sounded big, bold and gutsy, which was exactly the image they wanted. If Yorkie was a person they would be a lorry driver, while Dairy Milk is a creamy princess. With TV advertising, Yorkie took off and gave Cadbury a fright. They fought back by relaunching Dairy Milk, restoring the thickness and raising the price instead.

Did you know? Rowntree named the Yorkie after their York factory where it's made.

9. M&Ms

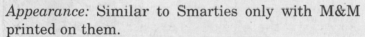

Born: 1940

Parent: Mars

Appearance: Similar to Smarties only with M&M printed on them.

In Britain there's Smarties, in America it's M&Ms. But since 1987 the American version has been catching on fast in Britain too.

How did Forrest Mars come up with candy-coated chocolate? The story goes that in 1937 he was travelling in Spain during the Spanish Civil War. Mars saw off-duty soldiers eating lentil-shaped, candy-coated chocolates. It was one thing he'd always dreamed of – a chocolate that wouldn't melt in the sun!

In America, M&Ms were launched as "the sweet that melts in your mouth not in your hand." (Minstrels made the same claim in Britain.) Mars says M&Ms stands for Mars (so good they named it twice.) In fact it was originally Mars and Murrie. Bruce Murrie was a partner in Mars' chocolate empire but he soon found it impossible to work with Forrest Mars. If Mars didn't like the sales sheets Murrie provided, he would scrawl FAILED on them and flush them down the toilet! Murrie eventually resigned but his initial still appears on the coloured candy.

Did you know? When they launched M&Ms in Italy, people thought they were…

10. Double Decker

Born: 1976
Parent: Cadbury

What makes a new chocolate bar a hit? Is it a wonderful new flavour or some amazing new ingredient like rhino horn? Actually, it's neither. The best loved chocolate bars, according to research, are

ones that don't taste too different from anything else. It sounds barmy but what people like is a familiar, boring flavour as bland as baked beans. So when Cadbury launched Double Decker they didn't put anything new into the mixture. Nougat, cereal and chocolate – all tried and tested ingredients. They just changed the texture a little and, lo and behold, Double Decker was a roaring success. So next time you're dreaming of inventing a pickled-onion-flavoured choc bar, think again. Try something unexciting – like baked bean flavour.

Did you know? In its first year of sales, Double Decker entered the confectionary charts at number 25. Sitting pretty at number one was the Mars bar.

AH, HERE COMES THE NUMBER 25

The man from Mars

Forrest Mars, the man who gave his name to the Mars bar, died on 2 July 1999. It would be nice to say he was a dear old man who just wanted to make children happy. It would be nice but untrue. According to those who knew him, Mr Mars lived on another planet from most people.

Here's a few strange but true facts about the man from Mars.

1. Workers in the Mars factory had to wear freshly cleaned uniforms every day. Woe to anyone with the tiniest speck of a chocolate stain on their uniform. Mars fired them on the spot.

2. Nice Mr Mars once hired private detectives to dig up dirt on his stepmother's family. Why? So he could get his sticky hands on his father's chocolate company in America.

3. On finally taking over his dad's business, Forrest began his first meeting with a prayer. Sinking to his knees on the carpet he began:

I PRAY FOR MILKY WAY, I PRAY FOR SNICKERS...

...and so on through all 26 products.

4. Mars once taught one of his company bosses a lesson by giving him a plate of Pedigree Chum dog food. (Not many people know Mars Inc. runs a vast pet food empire that accounts for half of its sales.) "It's part of your duties to sample the food," Mars told him. Did the boss quit? No, he swallowed his pride along with a large chunk of dog food.

5. In the 1970s, Mr Mars lived alone above his Las Vegas factory. He had two-way mirrors installed in his office so that he could keep an eye on his workers.

6. Miserly Mars' American factory turned out millions of candy-coated M&Ms – but his own kids never got a single one of them. He said the bright buttons couldn't be spared. He needed every last one!

Triffic trivia: Mars bars

If Mr Mars was an oddball, the stories about his most famous creation are no less weird. No other chocolate bar makes the news as regularly as the Mars bar.

1. Food watchdogs attacked the Mars advertising slogan in 1991. "There is no scientific evidence that Mars makes any positive contribution to working, resting or playing," they said. But the Independent TV Commission ruled that Mars could keep their slogan.

2. After a fierce blizzard four British skiers were stranded for six days on Russia's Mount Elbus. They stayed alive by eating Mars bars.

3. Film stars Elizabeth Taylor and Joan Collins and footballer Paul Gascoigne share one thing in common - their passion for Mars bars.

4. An art student once sculpted 150 Mars bars into a giant chocolate tongue at Cheltenham and Gloucester College of Higher Education.

5. Though sweets were rationed during the Second World War, the American government ruled that Mars bars were essential supplies for their troops.

6. The Financial Times has described the Mars bar as "a currency for our time". Because it contains staple foods such as cocoa, milk, vegetable fats and sugar, it's a more reliable currency than gold, which is prone to speculation.

7. Mars can save your life! When diabetic Jess Yates felt himself slipping into a coma he waved a Mars bar wrapper under his dog's nose and said, "Fetch." The dog obeyed and the sugar in the bar revived his master.

8. From start to finish a Mars bar takes two hours to make.

9. British Rail trains travelling in remote parts of Scotland used to keep Mars bars in their emergency packs in case they were cut off by snow.

10. In 1991, when the Mars bar was launched in Russia, queues were so long that each person was only allowed to buy four bars.

The bars that bombed

Names like Mars bar, Kit Kat and Crunchie will be familiar to you unless you happen to be a chocolate-deprived alien just landed from outer space.

But what about choc bars like Whistler, Skippy or the delightful-sounding Skum Banana? These names surely deserve their own top ten because they're the great chocolate flops of all time – bars that were launched with high hopes but sooner or later came to a sticky end.

Top of the flops

1. Marz bar

In 1933 the new Mars bar was so popular that shops couldn't get enough of them. So one cheeky shopkeeper in Glasgow came up with a solution. He made his own and called it the Marz bar. Clever, eh? The Scottish version was, of course, cheaper and thinner (and probably yukkier) but it was sold in an almost identical brown wrapper to the original Mars. It landed the cheeky Scots trader in court. When questioned, he claimed, "We always say it's our own make when we sell a Marz bar." He probably also claimed to be in close touch with the Loch Ness monster.

ACTUALLY, IT'S THE LOCH NEZZ MONSTER

2. Oak Tray

You've heard of Cadbury's Milk Tray chocolates (1915) but what about the not quite so successful Oak Tray launched in the 1920s? Chocolates with a woody flavour? No, they just came in a clever box that looked like an oak tray. Sadly they didn't take root. Well they woodn't, wood they?

3. FREAK Chocolates

If Oak Tray didn't take your fancy there was always Freak Chocolates from America. The novel idea was to mix in a few freaky centres along with the normal ones in the box. And just to make it harder the shapes of the chocs didn't give you a clue. Instead of biting into caramel you might find yourself sucking on an olive or gherkin-flavoured centre or a cheese cube chocolate. Mmm, can't think why they didn't catch on!

4. CHOCOLATE APPLE

Terry's Chocolate Orange is an invention that's still with us today. But did you know that Terry's first fruity idea was the Chocolate Apple? It lasted for 20 years until the 1950s, so for a flop it was actually a modest success.

5. RADIOACTIVE CHOCOLATE

No kidding, Radium Chocolate was sold in Germany during the 1930s. In those days, radioactivity – the deadly stuff you get from nuclear waste – was thought to be good for your health! So the German makers added radium salts to their chocolate bar and told customers, "Eat this and feel great." British chemists weren't convinced – they nicknamed it the "Suicide Bar".

6. Whistler

Launched by Cadbury with a great fanfare in the 1970s, Whistler was "one of the most thoroughly researched brands ever introduced by the company". It was also an almighty flop.

CALL THAT A GREAT FANFARE!

7. NUNCH

Another bright idea from Cadbury. This blend of coffee and walnut was promoted as the "nunchiest bar ever". Catchy but what the nunch did it mean? Nunch ended up in the dustbin with the other flops.

8. inca

Despite the fact that Cadbury's Aztec bar bit the dust in 1978, Rowntree still believed the idea of harking back to the dawn of chocolate's nutty history was a winner. They came up with Inca, offering no less than three flavours – roast hazelnut, walnut and (probably a mistake) apricot truffle. Predictably, Inca was a stinker and went down the pan.

9. MINT CRACKNEL

If ever a chocolate should have succeeded it was Rowntree's Mint Cracknel. The idea for spinning the strands of the sugar centre was copied from the manufacture of nylon.

Mint Cracknel was fiendishly clever but that didn't prevent it from being a flop.

10. SKUM BANANA

The search for the perfect name for a chocolate bar goes on – but we can safely say Skum Banana isn't it. It was marketed in Britain in the 1980s by an Italian firm who wholly failed to understand British tastes.

The bar's the star

The twentieth century has been called the age of technology, but actually everyone knows it was the age of the chocolate bar. Before the 1930s chocolate meant a bar of plain solid chocolate. Then chocolate-makers had the bright idea of putting a filling inside the chocolate. Soon they were playing with the shape and texture and before long, a tidal wave of chocolate novelties was released on the world.

Chocolate with caramel, coconut, nougat or wafer; chocolate in bubbles, flakes or swirls; chocolate in balls, triangles or squares – the variations were endless. And our appetite for new chocolate bars is still just as strong in modern times. In the 1970s alone Mars, Cadbury and Rowntree launched 44 new chocolate products (30 of them flopped so badly they were quickly withdrawn). The search goes on to create another Mars Bar or Kit Kat that will become a new classic to tingle the world's taste buds.

Having met the tops and the flops, you may wonder how a new bar is invented. Are there teams of eggheads in secret laboratories experimenting with chocolate at this very moment? And how does a new bar make it from the idea stage into your sticky hand?

Read on to find out how a bar is born...

A BAR IS BORN-
HOW TO SELL CHOCOLATE

So you want to market a new chocolate bar and make a million. How do you go about it?

You could:

① STEAL SOMEBODY ELSE'S IDEA AND DISGUISE IT AS SOMETHING NEW

NEW!

PORKIE BAR

IT'S GOT A SAUSAGE CENTRE!

② CHUCK IN ANY INGREDIENTS YOU CAN FIND AND SEE HOW IT TURNS OUT

ANYONE SEEN MY SANDWICHES?

③ GET SOMEBODY IN THE PUBLIC EYE TO PROMOTE YOUR NEW CHOC BAR

HERE IS THE NEWS... IT'S YUMMY, IT'S SCRUMMY AND IT'S HEADING FOR MY TUMMY

YUM

But the truth is that your chances of success are slim. Better make that wafer thin. For every 100 ideas for new chocolate bars only one will ever get made. What you need is a master-plan to make sure your bar is one of the rare winners. Every choc bar that makes it to the shops has to go through a seven-stage process from the first idea to the big launch. Follow these seven steps and you just might hit the jackpot.

Step 1: The choctastic idea

Chocolate-makers get their new ideas from two different departments. It might come from:

a) The marketing department.

b) The white-coated eggheads known as chocolate scientists.

The marketing department spot new opportunities for products.

For instance, Mars were the first to launch fun-size bars when they found out that mums were cutting up Mars bars into small slices for their children. Of course, they could have made a ready-sliced Mars bar, but that would have been too easy.

Meanwhile the eggheads in the labs are constantly experimenting with new things that can be done with chocolate.

Every now and again they invent a machine that can do something new with chocolate – fold it, ripple it, curl it – the possibilities are endless.

Eventually the new idea is born.

Step 2: The recipe

The new bar needs two things to make it to the next stage. It has to be unique – something that rivals can't easily copy – and it has to be the right price.

Product teams get to work on perfecting the recipe. Sometimes they'll have as many as 30 attempts to get it right.

Problems may crop up at this stage. In the case of one bar, the wafer kept going soggy, while another was spoiled by the raisins sinking to the bottom. Both these went in the bin. If the bar is too expensive to make it will also get thrown out, because price is all important in the chocolate market.

DIME BAR | DOLLAR BAR | 57 DOLLAR BAR

This experimental stage can take anything from six months to two years. You'll need lots of patience.

Step 3: The testing

Test, test and test again is the chocolate-maker's motto. So testing will actually take place at nearly every stage of the process. Being a chocolate tester sounds like a top job. Would you like to apply? As it happens market testing is done by ordinary customers like you and me. Groups around the country are invited to taste the new bar and say whether it's yummy or yukky. Sometimes several recipes will be tested. Think you've got what it takes?

Dear Mr Nestle,
I'm wild about chocolate
and my dad says I've got the
biggest mouth in our family.
Can you give me a job as a
chocolate tester? I don't
mind if you don't pay me,
as long as I can take my
work home.
    Yours hopefully
        Tracey Potter
            (age 9)

Step 4: The wrapper

The wrapper of the new bar is almost as important as what's inside. Classics like **Kit Kat** and **Mars** have eye-catching wrappers that stand out from the crowd. The packaging will also reflect who the bar is aimed at. A bright red and yellow wrapper will probably mean the bar's aimed at teenagers. Blue is usually aimed at adults who are willing to pay a higher price for something more sophisticated.

Any bar will have to compete with 50 other brands on the shelf, so the wrapper needs to get you noticed. Naming your chocolate bar is equally crucial. It has to give the right image.

Step 5: The adverts

No matter how scrummy a chocolate bar is no one will buy it if they don't know about it. That's where advertising comes in. Most bars are launched both on TV and in the press. The first question to ask is what message you want to give about your bar.

Is your bar a snack or a luxury? Is it smooth and silky, or a wacky, nutty kind of guy? Those are the kind of things you need to decide. An advertising company will make a number of adverts and you choose the best one.

This stage can cost up to around £4 million, so you'll need a big piggy bank.

Step 6: The test launch

You might think you're ready to hit the shops now, but no, first there's the test launch. This usually takes place in one region of the country for up to a year. It's the last chance to make sure you've got everything right. Is the name really as catchy as you think it is? Will those bits of bubble gum in the bar *really* be popular? Now's the time to find out.

Step 7: The big day

Roll of drums, fanfare of trumpets, the big day has arrived – your bar is finally in the shops. Maybe customers will be queuing round the block to get their hands on it, or maybe it will make a swift journey to the chocolate graveyard.

One word of warning – many bars do well at first but sales have to be sustained over a long time. Remember, nine out of ten products fail and join the ranks of the chocolate flops. But you never know, yours just might be the one in ten that's a success.

A bar isn't born overnight. As you'll have gathered, it's a long process to achieve success. But even with a success story things can sometimes go unexpectedly wrong. Take the case of a well-known Cadbury's bar that's still around today. Can you guess its name?

The bar that was too popular

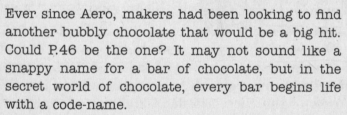

TOP SECRET REPORT

Code name: P.46

Mission: To grab part of the market cornered by Rowntree's Aero.

Date: 1981

Ever since Aero, makers had been looking to find another bubbly chocolate that would be a big hit. Could P.46 be the one? It may not sound like a snappy name for a bar of chocolate, but in the secret world of chocolate, every bar begins life with a code-name.

P.46 set out to be "young, active, trendy and convenient". As well as cool, it was a bubbly kind of character. A number of names were tossed into the melting pot: Rondo, Vista, Rollers, K.O. (or should that be OK?). What was needed was something light and frothy sounding.

Every step of the bar's development was kept top secret. All reports and designs for the new bar were shredded in a machine and then burned to make doubly sure. Who could tell if a spy from Mars might be hiding in Cadbury's dustbins to steal the recipe? As the long-awaited launch day approached, the bars were packed in plain boxes and driven in unmarked vans. Not a whisper about the new chocolate bar had leaked out.

The bar was test-launched in the north-east of Britain. People loved it. In fact, they loved it too much. Cadbury were churning out half a million of the new bars a week but it wasn't enough. Newspapers reported punch-ups in the shops as customers tried to grab the last precious bars on sale.

After only eight weeks it happened. P.46 had to be withdrawn – Cadbury simply couldn't meet the huge demand.

Despite the set-back, two years later the secret was out and the bubbly bar was re-launched to the whole nation. In its first year it rose to number three in the best-selling choc charts. P.46 was Cadbury's biggest hit of the 1980s. But what was its real name?

Answer:
Wispa. (Did you spot the a clue in the story?)

Cadbury still has its Wispa department today. The Wispa plant makes 1,680 bars per minute with each of the tiny air bubbles exact to within 0.2–0.3 mm. Do the staff have to whisper when they enter the Wispa department?

SHH! THAT'S TOP SECRET

Often chocolate companies pay well-known celebs to promote their new choc bars. Wispa featured in 40-second TV commercials using stars of well-known sitcoms from the 1980s. But sometimes a new bar gets unexpected backing from a different kind of celeb. Famous explorers, for instance.

The Daily Guzzle 7 January 1997
BRIT EXPLORER BITES NEW BAR

British explorer Sir Ranulph Fiennes has ordered 300 bars of a new chocolate bar to take with him on an expedition to Alaska. The new bar, Cadbury's Fuse – a blend of raisins, peanuts, cereal and fudge wrapped in chocolate – is "perfect" for expeditions, says Fiennes. "It is high in calories and low in weight. We usually take Dairy Milk chocolate, but at sub-zero temperatures it is like biting a rock. Fuse might be better on the teeth," said Sir Ranulph.

Great Scott!

Chocolate has long been a favourite nibble for dare-devil explorers. In 1911 Captain Scott took "cocoa and chocolate equipment" supplied by Fry for his doomed attempt to conquer the South Pole. Tragically, Scott never came back – and neither did his chocolate.

Nevertheless, Fry were keen to supply chocolate to any explorer with a compass and a pair of goggles. Alcock and Brown were said to be nibbling Fry's Vinello chocolate bars as they became the first men to fly across the Atlantic.

Best bite?

But what is the best choc bar to have in your back pocket when you're scaling Everest or toiling through the swamps of the Amazon? Over the page, follow our explorer's guide to the best choc bars – as tested by Sir Ranulph himself.

The Explorer's Guide to Chocolate

Fuse	Superb taste whether hot or cold. The best energy per bar for its weight.	9/10
Double Decker	Good energy per bar and clear list of contents.	8/10
Mars	Satisfying but much too runny if hot and very bad form on teeth if cold.	6/10
Picnic	Good. Has an unusually high energy content.	5/10
Snickers	Nice if you love peanuts, but it isn't such a complete meal.	4/10
Kit Kat	Too bland, especially if the bar gets cold. Not filling enough and not portable - breaks in pocket.	2/10

Ads and fads

Chocolate manufacturers spend millions a year on advertising their products. The chances are you've watched a TV advert for chocolate this week. Did you know 60% of chocolate buying is done on impulse? You see chocolate in a shop and you're suddenly overcome with a craving to eat some. But there are over 50 bars to choose from – so how do you decide which one? That's where adverts come in. If you've just watched a Crunchie advert you may find yourself strangely drawn to the idea of honeycomb in smooth chocolate.

Advertisers like to give choc bars catchy slogans. How many do you know?

Triffic trivia quiz

Can you match the chocolate bar to the slogans past and present?

1. Have a break, have a…
2. A … a day helps you work rest and play.
3. The crumbliest, flakiest chocolate.
4. Full of Eastern promise.
5. So delicious they're doomed.
6. Everyone's a fruit and nutcase.
7. A break from the norm.
8. Chunky chocolate.

Answers:
1. Kit Kat. **2.** Mars. **3.** Flake. **4.** Fry's Turkish Delight. **5.** Astros. **6.** Cadbury's Fruit and Nut. **7.** Twix. **8.** Yorkie.

Wacky adverts

Chocolate companies will go to any lengths to get their products noticed. No stunt is too crazy or too expensive. (Every year Rowntree spend over £3 million just persuading us to buy Smarties!) But some ads are smarter and more successful than others. If you want to make a big splash in the world of chocolate, take a few tips from these ideas.

1. Enlist the army

During the First World War chocolate was scarce in Britain. The British regiment who got sent a one ton crate of bullseyes must have looked across enviously at their Belgian allies who were scoffing chunks of delicious Toblerone. "As supplied to the Belgian Army" boasted Tobler on its adverts.

2. Rent a hunk

To promote their new Yorkie bar in the 1980s, Rowntree paid a hunky TV actor to take a bite in their TV adverts. He was so popular with female viewers that Rowntree had to set up a whole department just to cope with the demand for pin-up photos.

3. Rent a royal

In the days before the British royal family got a bad press, nothing did more for sales than the royal seal of approval. In 1921 Queen Mary herself visited Needler's chocolate factory and even tried her hand at making chocolates. Soon after, Needler's rushed out a Royal Taste Assortment, hinting that customers could hope to taste one of Her Maj's own efforts.

4. Star in a blockbuster movie

In 1981 Mars turned down one of the biggest scoops in advertising. Universal, makers of the blockbuster film *ET*, contacted the company. They wanted a scene in the film where the cuddly alien would be lured out of the woods by a trail of M&Ms. Mars said no and the starring role instead went to Hershey's Reese's Pieces. The movie broke box office records and sales of Reece's Pieces tripled within two weeks. Mars must have been under the moon.

5. Dig for gold

Another clever promotion invited customers to crack the Cadbury's Creme Egg mystery. To crack the mystery you had to buy a book which began with the tantalizing rhyme:

"Somewhere in the British Isles
Set apart by many miles
Twelve caskets lie beneath the ground
In each a scroll with ribbon round.
Upon each scroll to you is told
That you shall own an egg of gold..."

The golden eggs were worth finding. Each was valued at £1,000.

Weird receipe: chocolate pizza

What would you like on your pizza – ham and pineapple? Mushrooms and pepperoni? Or how about yummy chocolate? Sweet pizza may sound odd but it's all the rage in America.

Ingredients:
180 g margarine
250 g sugar
1 teaspoon vanilla
380 g flour
60 g unsweetened cocoa powder
1/2 teaspoon baking soda
1/4 teaspoon salt
180 g of chocolate chips
120 g chopped hazelnuts
60 g mini-marshmallows
1 banana, thinly sliced
1 egg

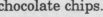

Method:
1. Beat together the margarine and sugar until it's light and fluffy. Blend in the egg and vanilla.
2. Combine the flour, cocoa, baking soda and salt. Add to the mixture and mix well.
3. Stir in half the nuts and about a third of the chocolate chips.

4. Place the dough on a lightly greased pizza pan, covered with foil. If it's a 30–35 cm pan it should spread to about 3–4 cm from the edge. Sprinkle with the remaining chocolate chips, nuts, marshmallows and banana.

5. Bake in the oven at 180°C (350°F) for 18–20 minutes or until the edges are set. Let it cool for ten minutes, then gently move it on the foil to a wire rack to finish cooling. (This is cold pizza!)

6. Add chocolate shavings as a final touch and cut into triangular wedges to serve.

Chocolate pizza is just one addition to the ever-growing range of ways you can eat chocolate. But the big business remains in chocolate bars. The UK chocolate market alone is worth £3.7 billion a year and is still growing. That's serious business for the big three chocolate companies – Mars, Cadbury and Nestlé-Rowntree. A story is told that at Nestlé-Rowntree a blazing argument in the boardroom was once interrupted by a secretary with the words:

"Only sweeties"? Try telling that to some of the wacky chocoholics you'll meet in the next chapter.

MAD FOR CHOCOLATE—WEIRD BUT TRUE STORIES

There are people who like chocolate.

People who *love* chocolate.

And people who NEED chocolate.

In this chapter we'll meet some of the weird people (and animals) who are *crazy* about chocolate.

At the beginning of the twenty-first century, chocolate has a huge impact on our lives. In the 1900s only the rich could buy chocolate at tea and coffee shops. Nowadays you'll find it in supermarkets, garages, cinemas, cafés – almost everywhere you go.

Chocolate has become as much a part of modern life as TV or computer games. Nine out of ten people in Britain eat chocolate and the figures are similar in America. So it comes as no surprise to discover there are many strange stories concerning chocolate. Perhaps you'll find some hard to swallow – but they're all perfectly true.

Record breakers

Every passion, from football to stamp-collecting, has its own record breakers. Chocolate is no different. If we're giving out medals these are the chocolate champions.

1. The top-selling choc

For the past ten years the world has scoffed more Kit Kats than any other chocolate bar. In 1995, for instance, we ate over 13 billion of them.

2. The biggest bar

In 1997, Cadbury created the world's biggest chocolate bar. It was a gigantic version of a Cadbury's Dairy Milk bar, 2.8 metres long and weighing 1.1 tonnes. Going by normal chocolate consumption, it would take the average person 100 years to chomp their way through the monster bar.

3. The chocolate-guzzling champs

A survey in 1998 put Britain top of the world chocolate-eating league. Brits chomp through 16 kg of choccie a year – on average that's about a bar a day. (We spend more on chocs than bread!) The Irish are equal top chocolate guzzlers, with the Swiss and Americans not far behind.

4. The oldest choc bar

I'M A HUNDRED AND THIRTY, YOU KNOW!

The oldest choc bar still available in the shops is Fry's Chocolate Cream. The grand old lady of chocolate first appeared in 1866. 130 years later Fry's Chocolate Cream is still for sale – though hopefully not the original bar or it'll taste a bit stale.

5. The oldest cocoa bean

The mother of milk chocolate is displayed in the Natural History Museum in London. The 300-year-old cocoa bean was found glued into the scrapbook of Sir Hans Sloane, a wealthy English doctor in the 1670s. Sir Hans may have created the first recipe for milk chocolate which later came into the hands of the Cadbury brothers.

GREAT! BUT HOW DO WE GET IT OUT OF THE DOOR?

6. The biggest Easter egg

A whopping Easter egg weighing in at 3,430 kg was made by Siegfried Berndt at his cake shop in Leicester, England in 1982. Siegfried's bumper egg was over 3 metres (10 feet) high. But even that was dwarfed by a monster 5.42 metre (18 feet) egg displayed in Belgium a year later.

7. The first choc-ice

Danish shopkeeper, Christian Nelson sold the first choc-ice in the USA in 1921. The idea struck him when an eight-year-old boy came into his shop and couldn't decide between a chocolate bar and an ice cream. Nelson combined the two and called it the "I-scream bar".

8. The worst selling chocolate

Proctor and Gamble, the American chemicals giant, once tried selling synthetic (artificial) chocolate. Yuk!

9. The most expensive chocolate

The costliest choccie you can't even taste. You can see it in a painting by the French impressionist Renoir called "Le Tasseau Chocolat" (the cup of chocolate). The painting shows a woman sipping chocolate and it sold at auction in 1990 for a cool £9 million.

10. The best wake-up choc

The first man to fly round the world solo was Willy Post in 1933. His marathon flight took seven days, 18 hours and 49 minutes. In order to keep himself awake the whole time he scoffed dozens of chocolate bars.

Now you know the oldest, the biggest and the best, but what about the weirdest? Here are some of the potty choccie stories that have appeared in newspapers in recent years.

The Daily Guzzle

CHOC SHOCK HORROR

Sweet-toothed mum, Merryl Baker, got a shock when she bit into her Galaxy bar – and it bit her back!

The 49-year-old mum found three teeth in her Double Nut and Raisin bar.

Merryl was tucking into the bar while reading the paper when she heard the crunch. "I couldn't believe my eyes. The sight of those teeth made me feel positively sick," said Merryl.

The mystery gnashers were sent to the Environmental Health department for analysis.

DOG IN HEAVEN

Spike the bull-terrier hit the jackpot when he dropped into his local supermarket for a snack. After wolfing down chocolate biscuits, staff locked the runaway dog in a storeroom – forgetting that it was full of Easter eggs. Spike was in chocolate heaven and gobbled £30-worth of eggs before his master, John Smith-son, arrived to collect him.

"Spike loves chocolate more than anything else, he can smell it from yards away," said 40-year-old Mr Smithson. The chocolate-crazy pooch is now in the doghouse.

CHOCOLATE WAR

After 25 years, peace has been declared in Europe's chocolate war. The battle over British chocolate has been raging since 1973 when the UK joined the European Community. The French and Belgians say British choccie is not the real thing because it contains a small amount of vegetable fat instead of using only pure cocoa butter.

Potty purists have demanded that English chocolate should be sold abroad as "household chocolate" or even "vegelate".

A spokesman for British chocolate replied, "We're not trying to tell the French and Belgians how to make their chocolate and they shouldn't tell us." So there!

The row was finally settled in 1999 when the EU ruled that English chocolate will be sold abroad as family milk chocolate. Anybody for vegelate?

CHAMPIONS LOSE THEIR MARBLES

What do you do if you've got no marbles to play with? Nip down to Tesco's and buy a few boxes of Maltesers, of course.

Contestants were stumped at the British Marbles Championships in Tinsley Green, Sussex, when their marbles got lost in the post.

The Maltesers proved to be the right size for marbles – if a little on the light side. When they were eventually replaced by practice marbles, the chocolates still found a use. "Players could eat them as their energy levels dropped," said organizer, Mr Sam McCarthy-Fox.

STUDENT GETS A TASTE FOR SCULPTURE

When art student Lisa Brown made a naked figure out of best white Belgian chocolate she was asking for trouble. Before she could exhibit her work of art at a show in London, a fellow student got his teeth into it. The hungry art-lover took a bite out of the figure's elbow when Lisa's back was turned.

"He told me that he bit the elbow instead of the bottom because that would be just too obvious. I think he's right," said Lisa who has decided to leave the missing bite as a comment on her art. And the title of the piece? "To Desire (Not Devour)"!

It's a disaster!

A gift of chocolates is meant to make somebody happy, but sometimes chocolate can land you in a whole heap of trouble, as these people discovered.

1. Drippy Cherry

When Mr John Cherry, editor of the *Seattle Times*, lost a libel case in court to Mrs Diana Lane, he agreed to settle the matter by allowing himself to be pelted with custard pies. Mr Cherry stood on the steps of the *Times* building wearing only a bathing-suit and a skin-diver's helmet. Since no custard pies could be found, Mrs Lane and her two sons, Fed (12) and Red (9), threw giant chocolate creams topped with Whippy Dip until the editor was coated from head to foot.

Mrs Lane's lawyer said, "I've had clients who got more money, but none who got greater satisfaction."

2. Santos in a Whirl

Roberto Dos Santos can never look at a Cadbury's Whirl again. He once left a Whirl in his lunchbox on a park bench in Willesden and had it stolen. That was bad enough, but with the chocolate were his life savings – which he never saw again.

3. Soft-centred thief

Neil Turley "borrowed" someone else's car and used it for a 350 mile jaunt across Britain. On returning the car to its place, he left a note saying he was sorry and a box of chocolates to replace the ones he'd found in the car and eaten. Sadly for Turley, the note was written on the back of a court bail form which gave his name and address.

Turley was given two years' probation and ordered to pay £20 for the petrol he'd used.

4. Unwelcome Topic

Marie Henriques was looking forward to eating the Topic bar she bought outside Piccadilly Circus station in London. But when she bit into it she got a nasty surprise.

"I took it out of my mouth and pulled the chocolate from around it," she said. "I found a grey furry-looking object." The object was the remains of a dead mouse which was later traced back to a nut factory in Turkey.

A Mars spokesman said, "We are shocked that proceedings like these could concern a Topic bar."

5. Dog's life for whippets

First it was athletics, now even the quiet sport of whippet racing is in the grip of a drugs scandal. The drug in question is the humble chocolate drop.

For years, chocolate has been a sweetie treat for racing dogs, but now the British Whippet Racing Association has banned the dogs from competition. Drugs tests have revealed traces of theobromine and caffeine in the doggy chocoholics. Owners of champion whippets, like Mark Pettitt, are furious. "Innocent people with pets who are just in this for fun are being branded drug cheats," he fumed.

6. Sweet spoon

It should have been one of the great inventions of all time. A chocolate spoon that would persuade kiddies to take their medicine. The aptly named Constance Honey came up with the sweet idea in 1937. But her idea flopped because it was just too popular. She would tell her young relatives: "I'd give you your medicine but I haven't got a spoon left in the house!"

141

And while we're on the subject of disasters, how about this contender for the world's most revolting recipe?

Weird recipe: chocolate ant crispies

Tired of jam tarts, fed up with flapjack? Try our delicious ant crispies. Creepy, crawly and irresistibly crunchy!

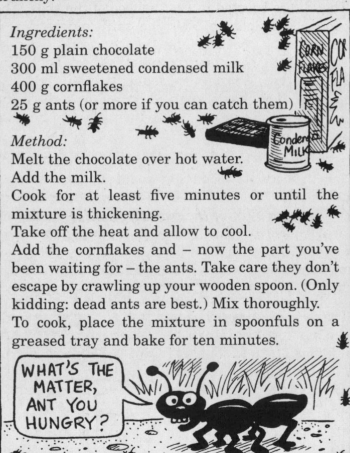

Ingredients:
150 g plain chocolate
300 ml sweetened condensed milk
400 g cornflakes
25 g ants (or more if you can catch them)

Method:
Melt the chocolate over hot water.
Add the milk.
Cook for at least five minutes or until the mixture is thickening.
Take off the heat and allow to cool.
Add the cornflakes and – now the part you've been waiting for – the ants. Take care they don't escape by crawling up your wooden spoon. (Only kidding: dead ants are best.) Mix thoroughly.
To cook, place the mixture in spoonfuls on a greased tray and bake for ten minutes.

WHAT'S THE MATTER, ANT YOU HUNGRY?

IT'S A CHOCOLATE WORLD!

"You see before you the result of a lifetime of eating chocolate."

Katherine Hepburn,
Hollywood film star.

The Aztecs boasted it was the food of the gods. The conquering Spanish took one sniff and kept it a secret for a century. The French royals liked to drink their *chocolat* for breakfast in bed. The English got a whiff of it and opened chocolate houses. The Swiss mixed it with milk. The Americans built machines to turn it out in bars by the thousand.

By the twentieth century chocolate had conquered the world – well almost.

"Perhaps 80% of the world's population has never eaten chocolate or drunk cocoa."

New York Times, 1979

That's a startling thought. But as far as the big chocolate-makers are concerned it just means there's millions of people out there waiting to discover the delights of triffic chocolate. Other countries have already tasted chocolate and discovered love at first bite.

USA
Americans eat about a quarter of the world's chocolate products. Yet Europeans scoff more chocolate per person.

Germany
Visit the famous chocolate museum in Cologne. Instead of buying a ticket you're given a chocolate at the door.

Switzerland
The Swiss remain among the world's champion chocolate eaters. Toblerone, meanwhile, is exported to over 100 countries.

Africa
75% of the world's supply of cocoa beans come from Africa.

Russia
Russians take chocolate as a luxury with tea. Smell the chocolate from Moscow's Red October factory - famous brands include the Happy Gnome and Peter the Great.

China
In 1980 a spy from the Swiss Suchard-Tobler firm unsuccessfully attempted to sell top-secret chocolate recipes to the Chinese.

Japan
Girls give their boyfriends chocolates on St Valentine's Day rather than the other way around.

India
For fifty years Cadbury has been a famous chocolate brand in India. They even have their own factory in the country.

145

Chocs in space

And it doesn't stop at the world, these days you can even eat chocolate in space!

A new rocket fuel developed at the University of Newcastle was inspired by the minuscule bubbles in Aero bars. Scientists say they could save $60 million on each Space Shuttle mission by using a fuel that has tiny air bubbles in its make-up.

Chocolate is the perfect high-energy food for space, say NASA scientists. But they've had to develop heat-resistant chocolate because there are no fridges in rockets.

Feast days

You have to hand it to chocolate-makers. Not only do they persuade the world that chocolate is part of a normal daily diet, but they also set aside special days of the year when we can binge on all the chocolate we can eat. Why? Because it's a festival of course!

Easter and St Valentine's Day were around a long time before chocolate, but manufacturers soon saw the chance to turn them into chocolate festivals.

Where would Easter be today without chocolate Easter eggs? And as anyone knows, chocolate and romance have always gone together. St Valentine must have had a sweet tooth.

Love potions

Down the ages many people have believed in the love-powers of chocolate. The Aztec emperor, Montezuma, you'll remember used to down a gold cup of chocolate before calling on one of his many wives. Later, that celebrated king of love, Casanova, boasted he drank hot chocolate rather than champagne. Nowadays romantics still give boxes of chocs to their sweethearts hoping they'll come over all weak at the knees. But is there any truth in the idea that chocolate is a love potion? Daft as it sounds, it's possible. Let's return to our chocolate scientist.

It's the PEA in the chocolate that's responsible. PEA is short for phenylethylamine, which, remember, is one of the 300 chemicals in chocolate. According to scientists, when you win the lottery or fall in love your PEA levels rise. So it's possible eating chocolate could reproduce the same feelings as falling in love. Of course, it's only a theory but millions of people who buy Black Magic on St Valentine's Day can't be wrong, can they?

Easter is egg-shaped

Eggs have been given as gifts for centuries – the Chinese were painting them 3,000 years ago. In the fourth century, eggs were forbidden food during Lent, so Christians started giving decorated eggs as gifts on Easter Sunday, when Lent was over.

Chocolate Easter eggs weren't thought of until the

nineteenth century, with France and Germany taking the lead. The first sweet eggs were solid chocolate and would have taken quite a while to gnaw your way through. Later, the Victorians popularized eggs in all kinds of novelty lines, such as real eggshells decorated with chocolate piping and marzipan flowers. By the 1920s chocolate had pretty well taken over – and eggs were only half the story. Enter a sweet shop at Easter time and the choice was totally mind boggling.

Rowntree, not to be outdone, had a 16-page catalogue for Easter which even included a truck which would pull into your model railway station carrying its Easter egg cargo. Sadly nothing quite so exciting exists today, though that won't stop us tucking into a Mars or Crunchie egg this Easter.

Have you ever wondered why some chocolate eggs have that crazy paving pattern on them? It's because in the early days some makers couldn't get their eggs to look smooth and round. Some clever clogs invented the scaly pattern to cover up the imperfections in the egg!

Weird recipe: fried Mars bar

You can always find a Mars egg at Easter but what about a weirder way to enjoy your favourite chocolate bar? Scotland is after all the land that gave us the haggis so it's fitting that it should have invented the equally daft Mars bar in batter. (Haggis, in case you don't know, is the delicious heart, lungs and liver of a sheep mixed with other ingredients and boiled like a sausage in the sheep's stomach. What's the matter – lost your appetite?)

Oddly, the fried Mars hasn't yet caught on else-where – but just give it time.

(Warning: if you're potty enough to actually try this recipe, ask an adult to help you.)

Ingredients:
Mars bars
groundnut oil
100 g plain flour
1 egg
300 ml milk
a bowl of flour

Method:
1. Make the batter by adding the egg to the sieved flour. Add a quarter of the milk and mix. Then add the rest of the liquid and beat until smooth.
2. Heat the oil to a temperature of 180°C (350°F). Careful, that's dead hot.
3. Using a slotted spoon dip the Mars bar into the batter, then the flour, then the batter again.
4. Now the cooking. Be warned, the Mars bar will cook in about 30 seconds. If you leave it too long it will melt and you'll have a sticky, gooey mess on your hands. As soon as the batter is golden and crisp take it out.
5. Eat when cooled and you're feeling brave.
NB A customer who tasted a fried Mars bar for the first time said: "It's pretty sickly... Kids will love it." What more can you say?

Triffic trivia quiz

True or false?

1. During World War Two the Cadbury factory made gas masks instead of chocolate.

2. A man in the 1720s lived for 30 years on a diet of only soup, biscuits and chocolate. He lived to be 100.

3. Quality Street chocolates, launched in 1936, were named after a play by JM Barrie, the author of *Peter Pan*.

4. Writer Roald Dahl used to test the chocolates in the nearby Cadbury factory when he was a schoolboy at Repton.

5. The world's longest banana split was 1.6 miles long.

6. Forrest Mars studied the mixing of cement to learn how to mix ingredients for chocolate.

7. Marilyn Monroe used to keep her hair healthy by using chocolate shampoo every morning.

8. Too much sugar destroys the flavour of chocolate.

9. In New York you can get a bust of yourself made out of chocolate for $350.

10. Before the days of drugs testing, Olympic athletes were sometimes fed a Mars bar just before a race to give them that extra kick.

It's a chocolate future

What will happen to chocolate as we go into the twenty-first century? Will it continue to find new ways to boldly go where sweets have never gone before? Or one day will we find that – horror of horrors – there's no longer enough chocolate to go round?

Chocolate addiction

As we've said, the world is divided into those who like chocolate and those who *need* chocolate. (Those who turn up their noses don't count as they are obviously barmy.)

People who are seriously addicted to chocolate seem to be on the increase. Real chocoholics eat chocolate like they breathe air. Take 51-year-old Joy Moore from Kendal in England. Joy owns a sweet shop – which is just as well because all she ever eats is chocolate.

Joy's daily diet makes strange reading:

Breakfast:	*Bowl of hot chocolate.*
Elevenses:	*Home-made chocolate buttons.*
Lunch:	*Chunks of pure dark chocolate.*
	Orange peel dipped in chocolate washed down
	with hot chocolate.
Afternoon snack:	*More home-made chocs.*
Evening meal:	*Dark chocolate and tomatoes*
	dipped in chocolate.
	Sweet: Grapes dipped in chocolate and water.
Nightcap:	*Cocoa liqueur*

Judging by her diet you'd expect Joy to be a toothless two-tonne whopper. In fact, she's a slim 60 kg and never has toothache. Strange, but then so is Joy in some ways. Take the time she was invited to a fancy dress party – she went as a giant cocoa pod.

Joy did once try to give her passion up but she says she came out in a cold sweat and got the shakes.

Chocoholics like Joy are so common these days that one company has been working on a possible cure. They're called Diet Scent Plasters. The idea is you stick the scented plasters on your hand and whenever you feel the urge to eat chocolate, you just take a whiff. The sweet scent of tropical orchid is meant to cure your craving. Only one problem – a month's supply of patches costs around £30 so it's cheaper to go on pigging out on chocolate.

A chocolate famine

Maybe chocoholics won't need a cure because in the future they won't be able to get their hands on the stuff. A world without chocolate sounds as likely as a world without schools (but much less fun). But is the idea of a chocolate famine so far fetched?

In 1998 there was a warning to start stock-piling Maltesers. Two killer bugs were threatening the world's cocoa supply. The nasty-sounding black pod disease hit cocoa suppliers on the Ivory Coast of Africa. While in Brazil a fungus called Witches' Broom was casting its withering spell on the cocao trees.

It all added up to potential disaster. Things were so serious that bigwigs from Nestlé, Cadbury, Mars and Hershey actually got together to talk about the problem! (Normally they weren't even on nodding terms.) One New York restauranteur warned,

"We may be going back to the turn of the century where chocolate was the preserve of the rich. It could be a chocolate-free millennium."

That may sound like scare-mongering, but all the same, have you got enough Maltesers?

Chocolate: the final frontier

With the birth of the fried Mars bar, not to mention the ice-cream Twix, you might think chocolate inventions have gone about as far as they can go. You'd be wrong of course. As long as there are chocolate lovers out there, makers will continue the search for new ways to tempt our taste buds.

In the 1990s we had:

- chocolates stamped with hologram pictures

- chocolate that can withstand temperatures of up to 60°C (140°F). The hot choc was invented for US troops to eat during the Gulf War

- predictions that the next generation of chocolates may be designed by computers (and probably eaten by robots!).

What will the chocolate boffins dream up next?

One thing's for sure, the Aztecs started something that won't go away. Anyone who thinks the future is bright is wrong. The future is brown and its flavour is chocolate.